shaker-style
wood projects

ROBERT SONDAY

Ash Trestle Table. The table, made by Robert Sonday, is accompanied by a Swing Handle Basket by Stephen Zeh.

shaker-style wood projects

ROBERT SONDAY

STERLING PUBLISHING CO., INC. NEW YORK
A STERLING/CHAPELLE BOOK

Chapelle Limited

OWNER:
Jo Packham

EDITOR:
Leslie Ridenour

STAFF:
Joy Anckner, Marie Barber, Malissa Boatwright, Kass Burchett, Rebecca Christensen, Holly Fuller, Marilyn Goff, Amber Hansen, Michael Hannah, Shirley Heslop, Holly Hollingsworth, Susan Jorgensen, Susan Laws, Barbara Milburn, Karmen Quinney, Cindy Rooks, and Cindy Stoeckl

PHOTOGRAPHY:
Kevin Dilley, photographer for Hazen Photography; Jo Packham, stylist

Special thanks to the Shaker Village of Pleasant Hill for allowing us the use of their lovely facilities for our photography.

Library of Congress Cataloging-in-Publication Data

Sonday, Robert.
    Shaker-style wood projects / Robert Sonday.
        p.   cm.
    "A Sterling/Chapelle book."
    Includes index.
    ISBN 0-8069-1386-X
    1. Furniture making—Amateurs' manuals. 2. Shaker furniture––Amateurs' manuals. 3. Furniture—Reproduction—Amateurs' manuals.
I. Title.
TT195.S57 1997
684.104—dc20
                                        96-44348
                                           CIP

10 9 8 7 6 5 4 3 2

A Sterling/Chapelle Book

Published by Sterling Publishing Company, Inc.
387 Park Avenue South, New York, NY 10016
© 1997 by Chapelle Ltd.
Distributed in Canada by Sterling Publishing
℅ Canadian Manda Group, One Atlantic Avenue, Suite 105
Toronto, Ontario, Canada M6K 3E7
Distributed in Great Britain and Europe by Cassell PLC
Wellington House, 125 Strand, London WC2R 0BB, England
Distributed in Australia by Capricorn Link (Australia) Pty Ltd.
P.O. Box 6651, Baulkham Hills, Business Centre, NSW 2153, Australia
Printed in Hong Kong
All Rights Reserved

Sterling ISBN 0-8069-1386-X Paper
0-8069-1381-9 Trade

If you have any questions or comments or would like information about any specialty products featured in this book, please contact:

Chapelle Ltd., Inc.
P.O. Box 9252
Ogden, UT 84409

Phone: (801) 621-2777
FAX: (801) 621-2788

special thanks

FAMILY

Thanks to Emrich and Irene Sonday, my father and mother; to my wife, Sarah McCollum and to our cat, Potato, who watched us the whole time.

OWNERS

I would like to credit the families from which these pieces are borrowed. They have contributed to the celebration of the life of this valuable craft. Many thanks.

From the collection of Alice Cornell of Cincinnati, Ohio, came Kelly Mehler's Drop Leaf Table.

From the collection of Dr. and Mrs. Gregory A. Wiseman of Indianapolis, Indiana, came Kelly Mehler's Chest of Drawers.

From the collection of Joe and Suny Monk of St. Stephens Church, Virginia, came the Rocking Chair— Ladder Back with Finials.

From the collection of Norm Sartorius and Diane Bosley of Parkersburg, West Virginia came the purpleheart Rocking Chair— Woven Back with Shawl Rail.

Thanks to all of the families of the contributing furniture makers—for emptying their households so we could photograph their heirlooms.

ARTISTS

Silk and wool pillows pictured on pages 38 and 55 were made by Ann Brauer of Ashfield, Massachusetts.

Neil Colmer of Berea, Kentucky, made the Whig Rose Runner on page 96 and the Double Woven Rug on page 132.

The large turned wood object on page 14 is from the Black Pot Series by John Jordan of Antioch, Tennessee.

The Basket Rimmed Koa Bowl on page 78 was made by Charles Kegley of Pearland, Texas.

Charles Harvey, a featured artist in this book, also crafted the Oval Carrier pictured on page 112.

The Hardbound Books with Silk and Paste Paper on pages 117 and 120 were made by Julia Leonard of Penland, North Carolina.

The Ceramic Covered Vessel, atop the Corner Cupboard on pages 127 and 128, was made by Thomas Clarkson of Ruckersville, Virginia (the turned wood vessels inside the cupboard were made by the author).

Stephen Zeh of Temple, Maine, crafted the Swing Handle Apple Basket on page 123 and Covered Swing Handle Basket atop the Trestle Table on pages 32 and 74.

The Accent Mat atop the Trestle Table on pages 32 and 74 were made by Neil Colmer.

The Sugar Maple Burl Hat sitting on the Arm Chair—Ladder Back with Finials on pages 20 and 37 was made by Johannes Michelsen of Manchester Center, Vermont.

Porcelain vessels, Moss & Lichen and Flambe, atop the Chest of Drawers on pages 103 and 105, were made by Cliff Lee of Stephens, Pennsylvania.

SHAKER VILLAGE OF PLEASANT HILL

Special thanks to the Shaker Village of Pleasant Hill at Harrodsburg, Kentucky—especially Vivian Yeast and her friends who work at the Centre Family Dwelling—for allowing us the use of their facilities. It was such a wonderful setting for our photography.

The largest community of its kind, Pleasant Hill offers self-guided tours, riverboat excursions, shops where handmade crafts are sold, meeting facilities, and dining and overnight accommodations in original nineteenth-century buildings.

The village has 33 restored structures in their original location. It is operated as a nonprofit, educational corporation and income that is generated by the use of visitor services is contributed to the preservation of this National Historic Landmark.

FURNITURE MAKERS

Many thanks to each of the wonderful furniture makers in this book and to those I couldn't include for logistics' sake. It is reassuring to know you are all out there.

ROBERT SONDAY

contents

SHAKER-STYLE WOOD PROJECTS

"Let a stranger visit your country, and inquire... for your best specimens of agriculture, mechanics and architecture, and sir, he is directed to visit the Society of Shakers at Pleasant Hill."

—Robert Wickliffe, Senate of Kentucky, January, 1831.

✖ by way of introduction

The purpose of this book is to feature interpretive Shaker-style furniture and woodworking— examples made by living professional furniture makers for readers to admire, to consider buying, or to make a personal copy. These are pieces endowed with intent of a high level of quality, and a harmonious spirit.

"Interpretive" Shaker furniture, in this book, means work fashioned by a current maker that has, more or less subtly, evolved from the work of the Shakers, and is in keeping with the "Shaker style."

These pieces were conceived and made with as much thoughtfulness and centeredness as is evident in the Shakers' remaining effects.

I am happy to provide added celebration to the work of some well-known and excellent modern professional makers with the publication of this book. These professionals build a longer and deeper repertoire of pieces than can be represented here. Each maker is quite grounded in what the Shakers called being in "the world." Their feel for the Shaker effects is largely a meaningful, realistic, current-day grasp on the Shakers' simplicity, harmony, and efficiency.

These artists are trying to earn a living making pieces of great quality. It is difficult, if not almost impossible, to support oneself in this endeavor. However, these are modern-day furniture makers of great integrity—in the best sense of the profession. I would like to balance the hard work and good judgment of these gifted makers by continuing to put their work out to the world. ■

✖ the shakers

The Shakers were the largest and best-known communal society in nineteenth-century America. Their society began as an offshoot of the English Quaker church. They were a practical and successful people who found a peaceful way of life based on the tenets of celibate purity, confession of sins, separation from the world, and community of goods. They also believed in advanced social principles such as equality of race and sex and freedom from prejudice.

These characteristics, combined with the Shakers' unusual living arrangements or celibate "family dwellings," in which the men occupied one side of the dwelling and the women the other with strict laws of chastity keeping them separated, prompted suspicion, scorn, and ridicule from outsiders.

However, the society survived and prospered in the 1800s. Shaker colonies dotted new England, the Midwest, and the South. Out of these colonies came many labor-saving devices and agricultural innovations. The Shakers quickly earned a faultless reputation for quality in manufactured products.

Today there are less than 10 preserved and existing Shaker villages where the Shaker colonies once thrived. ■

shop basics

STATIONARY MACHINERY

Anyone attempting to make the pieces in this book should have these pieces of machinery:

A. Table Saw
B. Jointer
C. Band Saw
D. Drill Press, with a fully tilting table
E. Small Planer
F. Router Table
G. Lathe
H. Abrasive Planer

Optional pieces of machinery that improve the shop working conditions are:

A. Radial Arm Saw
B. Shaper
C. Vacuum Veneer Press
D. Edge Sander

To both of the above lists, add one piece of equipment that any shop should have—a dust collector. Whether it is a small mobile unit, or a large stationary one, it is a must for one's own health.

Also, depending on the amount of work to be done, look into purchasing a dovetailing jig, lathe duplicator, and slot mortiser, which lend themselves to production work.

HAND TOOLS

Anyone thinking of making furniture needs a good compliment of hand tools. Those listed below are the most commonly used.

- Handsaw, 10 pt.
- Dovetail Saw—European or Japanese
- Jointer Plane
- Block Plane
- Convex Plane
- Rabbet Plane
- Set of Chisels—⅛" through 1"
- Profile Gauge for curves
- Electric Hand Drill with a minimum of ⅜" chuck, variable speed and reversible
- Skill Saw for cutting sheet goods
- Saber Saw
- Dowel Centers
- Compliment of Sanders—belt, orbital, etc.
- Cabinet Scraper
- Oil or Water Stones
- Router with a compliment of bits
- Channel Lock Pliers
- Linesman Pliers
- Clamps—you can never have enough clamps—minimum needed is (12) 4' bar clamps, (6) 2' pipe clamps, and (12) 4" quick clamps

JOINERY

Places where certain joints work best are:

Dovetail: case and drawer construction, pedestal tables for attaching legs

Mortise and Tenon: doors, cabinet faces, tables, and chairs

Dadoes: insides of cabinets and drawers to hold dividers and bottoms

Rabbets: in cabinets to house backs and in combination with dovetails to form lipped drawer faces

Tongue & Groove, and Shiplap: allows pieces to expand and contract with the weather in backs of large casework

Dowels & Biscuits: where mortise and tenon is used, but lack the strength of mortise and tenon joinery

Lamination: 1) edge joining boards together to form larger pieces, such as table tops and door panels, or 2) gluing together relatively thin veneers or wood, over a form, to create bent wood pieces

Finger Joint: where dovetails are used, are commonly found in smaller boxes and drawers

Spline Miter: where a clean look of a miter is desired, but the added strength of the spline is needed. Note also that the spline helps line up the miter at assembly.

a bit of advice

SAFETY

Due to the inherently dangerous and complex nature of furniture making, professionals generally recommend in-person training through local course offerings. Supplement these courses by thorough study of the many excellent publications available on the subject of developing skills for furniture making and woodworking.

THE ART OF WOODWORKING

Check the actual piece-in-progress before drilling, sawing, planing or making any move that is irreversible. Ask questions such as "Does it fit, or did the actions of the woodworking machinery, sanding processes, tooling differences, and humidity dimension changes occurring overnight (or over the course of the construction period) mean that adjustments need to be made?" If any of these conditions have affected the piece, adjustments may be made in the instructions, dimensions, drill center points, markings, or some other element.

ALTERNATIVES

These pieces can be built as they are shown. However, it is not necessary to use the shapes, sizes, colors, or proportions exactly as they have been set forth in the instructions and drawings. Feel free to use other shapes and features that seem exciting. Those provided are to help the woodworker understand scale and proportion and thereby create a piece to the specifications that suit the individual with the good lines of fine furniture. In this manner the woodworker will create his own design language and thus, his own distinct work.

TECHNICAL ALTERNATIVES

There are a thousand and one methods to do any one step in woodworking. For the sake of clarity, only one method is given at each step in this book. However, this is in no way intended as the definitive method. The wood-worker is encouraged to suit his own technology appropriately, innovatively, economically and ALWAYS SAFELY.

WOODS

Substitute most any hardwood for those shown in each project, except the Oval Box (on page 97) which is fairly species-specific—Charles Harvey explains this in the instructions for the piece. One of the joys in the shop is the great selection of woods, since they are interchangeable in so many cases.

The odd figured piece of the otherwise calm-grained species such as cherry, walnut, or ash can often be found at the local lumber yard. The back splats in the Side Chair —Ladder Back with Finials (on page 26) are a great example. Just one board that didn't fit in with the rest produced all those splats.

Ask the lumber dealer what has been pulled aside that is special.

Building pieces from a single flitch, or consecutively cut log, is very satisfying. A marvelous example of this method is Kelly Mehler's matching Chest of Drawers on page 104.

Look hard at the boards while at the lumber yard and during the planing process. Matching can easily make the difference between a good piece and a handsome one. Bob Wurster planned his Corner Cupboard (on page 126) around two lovely featured boards, complementing an already exquisite design.

There is a greatly widened spectrum of natural colors from the lesser-known woods of the world, which have become available since the Shakers did their woodworking. Infusing some of these colors into the Shaker forms has always been a delightful process since they loved wonderful coloring. It is a relief that these newly available woods are beginning to be harvested sustainably with respect to the surrounding nature and native people. Years ago, woodworkers were not aware of any threat to the rainforest. Suffice it to say, I have always been, and will always be, looking for appropriate special species.

A favorite color of the Shakers was yellow, which is characteristic of the lesser-known wood pao amarillo—unless it is painted over or stained. Subsequently, making seating from it naturally came to mind. Some clients make a bold, playful statement by using fire engine red for the weaving in these yellow chairs. By contrast, pao amarillo can seem subdued, with brown or green weaving.

The lesser known wood chechen, in the Peg Rail (on page 89) is certified by the Smart Wood Program of the Rainforest Alliance to be sustainably harvested. Such certification by an accredited program is the highest and most desirable level, at this time, of wood use.

FORM MAKING

Forms should be made from as cheap a material as possible. Three-quarter inch CDX (construction grade plywood) works well. It is put together with waterproof glue and wears well.

It is necessary to take as much care in making the forms as the piece of furniture. The piece will suffer if the form is not right.

It is good, but not necessary, to cover the two mating surfaces with something to protect the outside laminate faces. One layer of scrap linoleum, which is available at floor covering shops, works well. If linoleum is used, always back off the curve lines by the thickness of the linoleum to mark the final cut lines.

ASSEMBLY

One good way to make a form is to transfer the curves of both faces of the lamination, and their end marks, onto the ¾" layers of plywood. Bandsaw out the curves ¹⁄₁₆" outside the line discarding the waste plywood from inside the two curve lines. On only one ¾" layer, sand the ¹⁄₁₆" off very carefully, exactly to the lines of the curves.

Glue and screw this finish layer onto another plywood layer, aligning the lines together. Use plenty of screws and glue when assembling—forms receive a lot of stress from clamp pressure. Rout off the ¹⁄₁₆" oversize on the new layer flush with the first. In the same way, glue and screw the next layer on and rout it flush. Repeat for as many layers as are in the form. Apply three coats of a non water-base sealer-type finish, such as urethane or lacquer to help in clean up of glue at the end of each laminating glue-up session.

MORTISING BOX

Mortising boxes need to be made to fit a particular lathe. They should be made so the router can clear the largest piece. It may be necessary to make several different lengths of mortising boxes, because, for example, the dovetails of a pedestal table post are much shorter than the set of mortises in a chair back post.

Stability is the main quality needed for the material. High grade plywood or MDF (medium density fiberboard) works well. Just as with forms, care should be taken during construction. The boxes need to be very square and straight to work. See Mortising Box pattern below.

FINISHING

Because of the many differing formulations of each category of finish, plus the fast forward march of chemical research and conversion to water-basing for environmental concerns, the instructions on the can of finish should be followed.

If new to finishing, try oil and wax first because it is the most forgiving. Always test a scrap piece first, no matter what the type of finish. Or take the piece to a professional finisher for lacquering or other finishes like many excellent, seasoned professional furniture makers do.

There are many good books devoted to in-depth treatment of finishing instructions. These provide, in appropriate detail, instructions for what to do, and also what to do when something goes differently from what was planned—which often happens. ∎

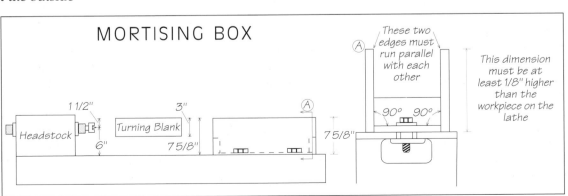

MORTISING BOX

1 1/2"   3"

Headstock   Turning Blank

6"   7 5/8"   7 5/8"

These two edges must run parallel with each other

This dimension must be at least 1/8" higher than the workpiece on the lathe

90° 90°

chapter 1

Robert Sonday:
Profile, Philosophy, & Projects

photo by D Wayne Blackdog

ROBERT SONDAY—A PROFILE
Robert Sonday is recognized by many of his peers in the woodworking field as an exceptional artist and craftsman. He is especially known for his work as a chairmaker and turner. His chairs are included in some of the finest residential and institutional furniture settings in the United States. Robert's work has also been featured in many galleries and museum exhibitions, including the Huntington Museum of Art in West Virginia, The Design Center in San Francisco, California, and the Sansar Gallery in Washington, DC.

Over the past several years, Robert has presented many workshops, demonstrating the fine art of his profession. In 1990, Robert was invited to Indiana University of Pennsylvania as an artist-in-residence. His residency was sponsored by the Mid-Atlantic Arts Foundation, supported by the National Endowment for the Arts. During his visit, Robert was especially generous in sharing his unique technical and design skills with each participant. His personal style of presentation was warm and always entertaining.

In 1993, Robert also presented a special lecture featuring his work, at the Cambria County Arts Center in Johnstown, Pennsylvania, on behalf of the traveling exhibition titled, "Woodturning as an Art Form: The Irving Lipton Collection."

As a fellow furniture designer, I have always been impressed with Robert's excellence of design and craftsmanship, especially in his high back chairs and rockers.

Similar in form to the classic slat-back chairs of the Shaker craftsmen, Robert's chairs are unique in their own way. His sensitivity to overall proportion, detail, selection of materials, and component shaping, express an extremely high level of individuality and refinement.

When you sit in one of his rocking chairs, you immediately sense the quality of "ergonomically correct" proportions. The position of the seat to the frame is stationed well, making it inviting and comfortable. The arm rests of the rocker are beautifully contoured and fitted into the front and back verticals, as well as perfectly sized for comfort and support of your arm. Push off and you are on your way to the perfect rock.

For the past six years, I have had the pleasure of sitting on one of Robert's rockers in my home just about every evening. As I sit with my coffee, rocking away the little worries of everyday life, I realize how important a well-designed chair can be for relaxing the body, mind, and spirit. ∎

—Christopher Weiland
Woodworking and Design,
Department of Art
Indiana University of Pennsylvania

ROBERT SONDAY —PHILOSOPHY

I strive to visually refine pieces to a scale in which they look light and welcoming, but retain the quality of being structurally sound. It is also very exciting to use the woods' own natural surprising colors to echo the paint and stain the Shakers used on their pieces.

Most of my work for the last 10 years has been Shaker chairs. I have created a design language of shapes in various parts of my chairs. These shapes re-occur in my non-seating projects too, resulting in a more harmonious group of pieces within a home.

The Shakers' reputation for quality in manufactured products gives us reassurance to pursue excellence, as is natural to do. And their affinity for developing the best, most innovative, practical and efficient technology is a clear example that inspires us to do the same. With the advantage of technology that has evolved since the Shaker's time, it has been most satisfying to make their designs more permanent structurally, and more comfortable anthropometrically. A chair shouldn't automatically need its rungs reglued every so many years. Rockers shouldn't eventually crack the posts of a beautiful bird's-eye rocker. Strength of grain direction should follow the curves of rockers. A complete spectrum of woods, such as those lesser known and certified sustainably harvested, shouldn't be unusable in Shaker seating because of construction constraints. I have reevaluated each detail on the furniture I've interpreted, solved these problems, and enjoyed the process. ■

ABOUT THE PROJECTS

You *can* do these projects. If you are eager to really apply yourself, then you will definitely have something to be proud of.

If you use the native ingenuity that resides in each person in approaching this type of furniture making, you'll be turning these instructions and drawings into physical reality. In our computer- and service-oriented culture, fewer people are comfortable making things. Except for you—right now! And don't flinch because there is no video accompanying this book to make the projects appear simple. Take heart—this is what being a furniture maker is all about. Part of the reason people buy books like this one is to experience what it is like to be a furniture maker, aside from being able to make and keep some of the projects. You will certainly gain this experience as you begin and complete even one of these projects.

As you begin a project, keep at it. Don't be fooled into thinking you are going to make good furniture in two days. This is a common misconception that has come about, again as a result of the information age, as some, proclaiming themselves to be master carpenters, have falsely implied that they are also master furniture makers. It requires more than two days, talent with a nail gun, and ownership of shop machinery to accomplish worthwhile furniture.

Furniture makers constantly battle this largely American mis-conception in their shops and in places they market their work. Those who have been misinformed are convinced that this endeavor takes little time, and that the only thing that sets furniture makers apart is that they own a shop (which can be quite a financial investment alone). Most established professionals dedicated their lives early on to the pursuit of excellence in furniture making. They have sacrificed much in the process including the many years required to perfect their skills to a respectable competence. Most of us are still growing even after a few decades.

ABOUT THE DRAWINGS

Most of the furniture makers featured in this book completed these pattern drawings long after the pieces were built so that you might have them for your reference. The actual pieces photographed were generally built almost without the aid of drawings. These professionals tend to hold many of the details somewhere inside themselves, mulling and reasoning and looking their way through the design and construction process. They often make the changes in response to the characteristics of the wood. There is always the possibility they might put down some sketches, a scaled view, or models to resolve specific unanswered questions, but the completed drawings in this book were completed for your sake. Enjoy them!

In all of my research of Shaker furniture and its historical reference materials, the one thing I did not see was original drawings of their furniture, which leads me to believe they didn't use drawings much either. It doesn't surprise me. ■

Petite pedestal. The curly maple Pedestal Table is a handsome accent to an open corridor.

Pedestal Table

by Robert Sonday

CONSTRUCTION

Select enough wood to glue up a square approximately 18½" x 18½". This wood will make the 18" diameter top.

Using the PTRS-2 pattern on page 17, trace the outline of the legs onto the leg blanks. Make the miter cuts at both ends of the leg stock blanks, and then cut out the rest of each leg. Sand to the line. Keep the waste stock from the leg blanks for test cuts when making the dovetails.

Mark 1¼" in from the ends of the legs where the dovetails will be cut. Taper the legs, stopping at the mark.

Using the PTRS-3 pattern on page 16, turn the post. Don't be afraid to make changes in the shape to suit individual taste.

On the lathe, turn the cylinder at the base of the post to a very consistent, exact 2¾" diameter over all 4" of its length. Take time in turning it.

Using the PTRS-4 pattern on page 17, set up the mortising box on the lathe, and rout the ¹³⁄₁₆" flats, just shaving the surface. Use a ½" straight bit first to waste away a ½" x ⅝"-deep groove under each of the three flats. Then set the dovetail bit to cut ⅝" deep, and make one pass cutting the dovetail.

Using the PTRS-5 pattern on page 18, and with the dovetail bit in the router table, make test cuts in the waste stock from the leg blanks. When the set up machines a good fit, cut the tails on the leg stock to fit the post. Chisel out the top of the groove in the post, so the legs slip up to shoulder where the taper starts. The widest part of each leg should protrude below the bottom of the post about ⅟₁₆". Make a mark on each leg where the bottom of the post comes. Drum-sand off the ⅟₁₆" or so below the mark, and smooth out the rest of the line with the drum sander, until the notch is gone. Glue the legs into the post.

Drill and countersink for the brass screws in the brass base plate, and attach the base plate with them to strengthen the dovetail joints.

Using the PTRS-6 pattern on page 19, cut out the top to 18⅛" round. Cut out the batten. Drill the 1"-o.d. hole in the batten to fit the tenon on top of the post. Taper the batten and then cut its ends round. Drill the screw holes for mounting the top.

Cut the wedge slot in the tenon. Put the batten hole over the post tenon. Make a wedge that will tighten the assembly as it is driven into the tenon. Disassemble these parts, and then assemble them with glue, and glue the wedge in fairly tightly. The tenon should be protruding ¼" above the batten. Trim it flush after the glue sets.

Shape the top by screwing a 6" face plate to the back of the top, and turning the edge to its profile. Sand the top. Screw the batten to the top.

Finish with two coats of oil and then one coat of wax.

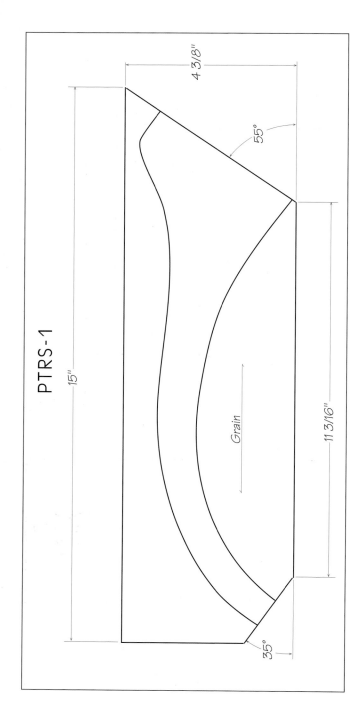

PTRS-1

15"

4 3/8"

55°

Grain

11 3/16"

35°

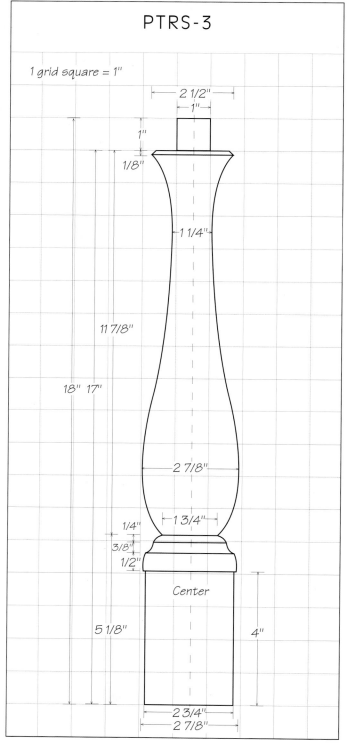

PTRS-3

1 grid square = 1"

2 1/2"

1"

1"

1/8"

1 1/4"

11 7/8"

18" 17"

2 7/8"

1 3/4"

1/4"

3/8"

1/2"

Center

5 1/8"

4"

2 3/4"

2 7/8"

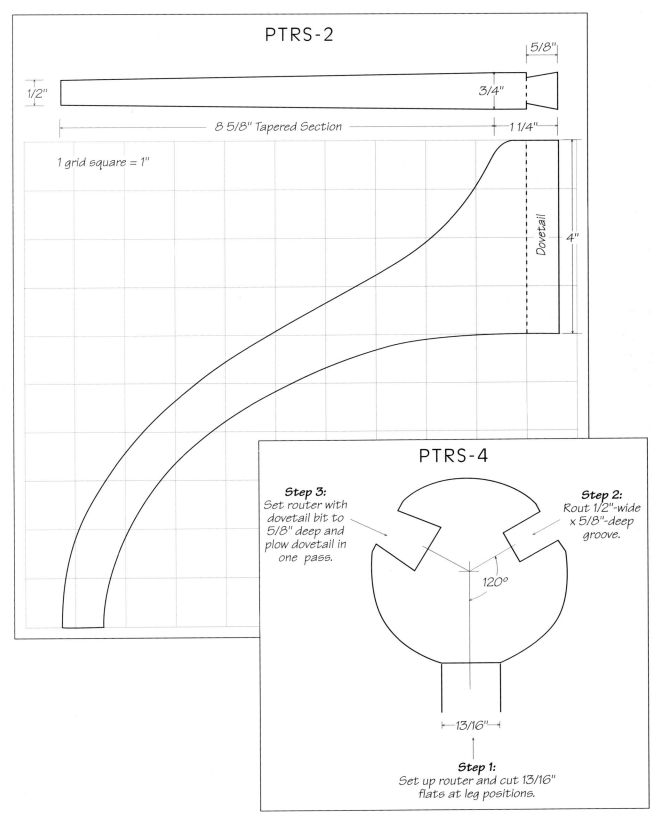

PTRS-2

5/8"

1/2"   3/4"

8 5/8" Tapered Section   1 1/4"

1 grid square = 1"

Dovetail   4"

PTRS-4

Step 3:
Set router with
dovetail bit to
5/8" deep and
plow dovetail in
one pass.

Step 2:
Rout 1/2"-wide
x 5/8"-deep
groove.

120°

13/16"

Step 1:
Set up router and cut 13/16"
flats at leg positions.

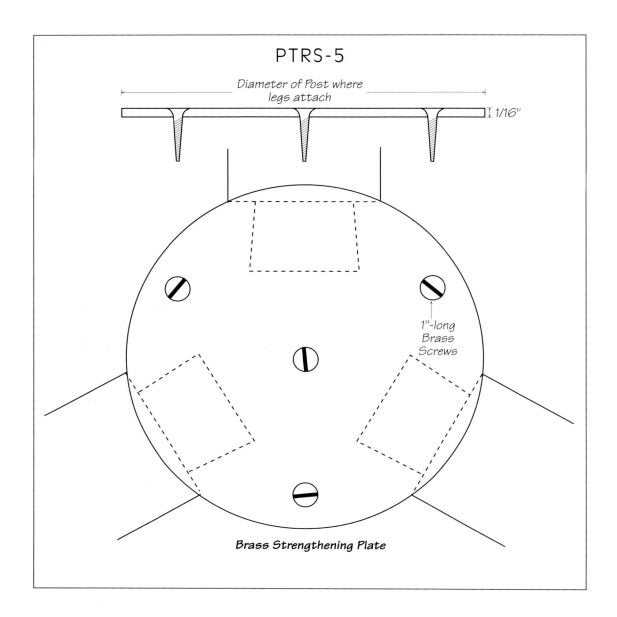

PTRS-5

Diameter of Post where legs attach

1/16"

1"-long Brass Screws

Brass Strengthening Plate

Most Shaker furniture makers avoided anything that resembled deception, including the use of veneer and grain painting (both of which made plain wood look finer and more expensive).

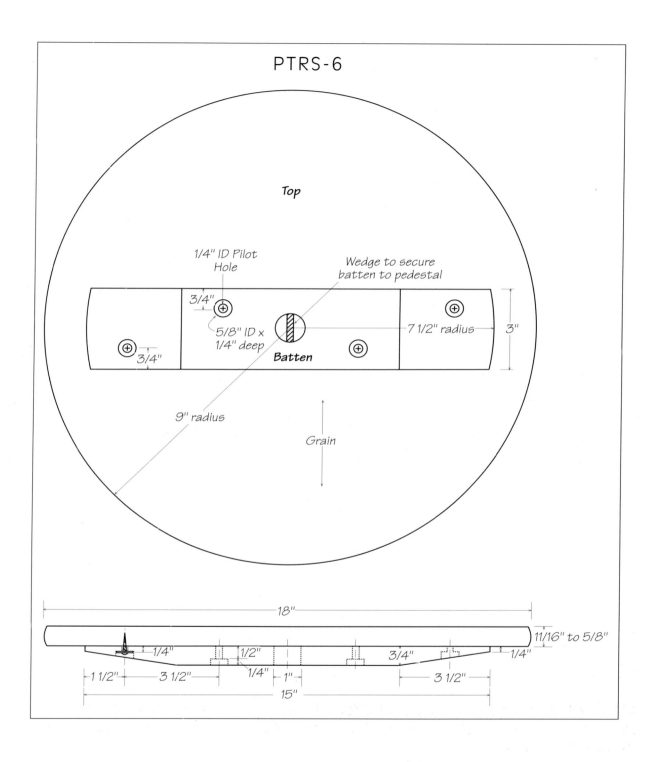

Top

1/4" ID Pilot Hole

Wedge to secure batten to pedestal

3/4"

5/8" ID x 1/4" deep

Batten

7 1/2" radius

3"

3/4"

9" radius

Grain

18"

11/16" to 5/8"

1/4"

1/2"

3/4"

1/4"

1 1/2"

3 1/2"

1/4"

1"

3 1/2"

15"

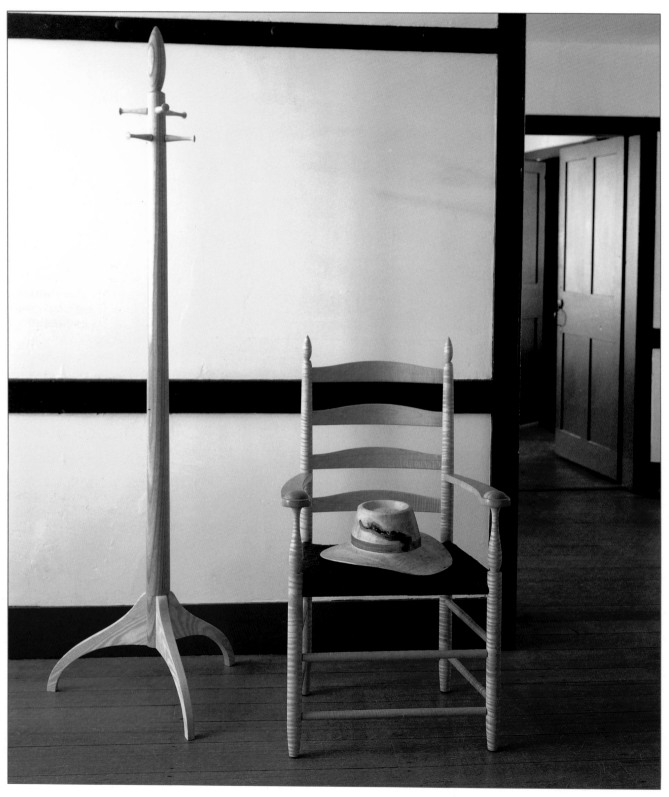

Coat check. The ash Coat Tree stands tall at the side of the Arm Chair—Ladder Back with Finials (instructions on page 33).

Coat Tree

by Robert Sonday

SPECIFICATIONS

BASICS
Material: ash
Overall Dimensions: 77" tall x 26" dia.
Finish: oil and wax

PART LIST
Ash

Post	(1)	3" square x 73⅜"
Pegs	(6)	1⁵⁄₁₆" square x 5½"
Legs	(3)	1⅛" x 6" x 18"

METAL & HARDWARE

Brass base plate	(1)	¹⁄₁₆" x 2½" dia.
Brass screws	(4)	1" long

CONSTRUCTION

Using the CTRS-2 pattern on page 22, trace the outline of the legs onto the leg blanks. Make the end cuts of 148° and 122° at either end of the leg stock blanks as shown on the CTRS-1 pattern, and then cut out the rest of each leg. Sand to the line. Keep the waste stock from the leg blanks for test cuts when making the dovetails.

Using the CTRS-2 pattern on page 22, mark 1¼" in from the large end of each leg where the dovetails will be cut. Taper the legs, stopping at the marks.

Using the CTRS-3 pattern on page 22, lathe-turn the post to a cylinder measuring 2¾" diameter x 73" long.

Turn a tenon 2" long x 2" diameter on the headstock end of the post. This will allow room later to get the router bit in to rout the dovetails.

Turn the cylinder down to 2½" diameter x 5¹⁵⁄₁₆", just above the tenon, for where the legs will attach to the post. This needs to be turned very straight to make the legs set right.

Turn the cylinder down at the tailstock end to a 2" diameter x 8" cylinder. This is where the finial will be turned later.

Set up a long tool rest and turn the taper in the post from 2¾" to 1⅞" over the 57¹⁄₁₆"-long section of the post. Finish-sand the taper to 320 grit. Turn down the 2" tenon at the head stock end to a ⅞" diameter to allow clearance for the dovetail bit.

Set up the mortising box on the lathe, and rout the ¹³⁄₁₆" flats, just shaving the surface. Use a ½" straight bit first to waste away a ½" x ⅝"-deep groove under each of the three flats. Then set the dovetail bit to cut ⅝" deep, and make one pass cutting the dovetail.

Lay out the peg holes and then drill them on the lathe with a drill guide mounted in the tool post holder of the lathe. Then turn the finial shape.

With the dovetail bit in the router table, make test cuts in the waste stock from the leg blanks. When the set up machines a good fit, cut the tails on the leg stock to fit the post. Chisel out the top of the groove in the post, so the legs slip up to shoulder where the taper starts. The legs should protrude below the bottom of the post about ¹⁄₁₆". Make a mark on each leg where the bottom of the post comes. Drum-sand off the ¹⁄₁₆" or so below the mark, and smooth out the rest of that line with the drum sander until the notch is gone.

Finish-sand the legs. Glue them to the post.

Using the CTRS-4 pattern on page 22, turn six pegs, according to instructions for Shaker Pegs on page 23. Slide the pegs into the post, then scribe them with a compass and cut the excess off with a carving tool to fit the contour of the post. Glue them in.

Drill and countersink for the brass screws in the brass baseplate, and attach the base plate with them to strengthen the dovetail joints as in PTRS-5 pattern on page 18.

Finish with two coats of oil and one coat of wax.

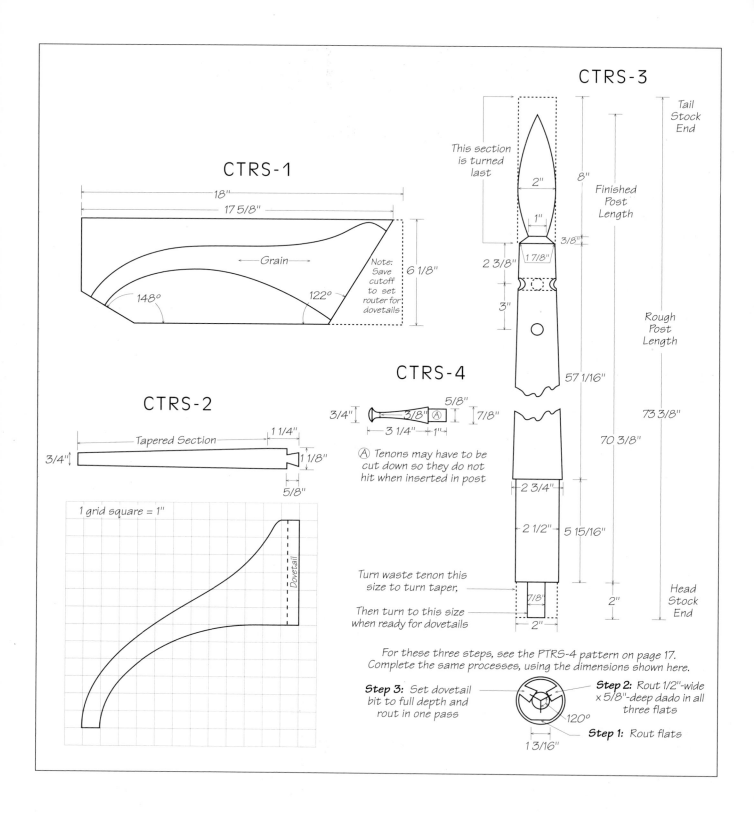

CTRS-1

18"

17 5/8"

Grain

Note: Save cutoff to set router for dovetails

6 1/8"

148°   122°

CTRS-3

This section is turned last

2"

1"

8"

Finished Post Length

Tail Stock End

3/8"

1 7/8"

2 3/8"

3"

57 1/16"

Rough Post Length

73 3/8"

70 3/8"

CTRS-4

3/4"   3/8"   (A)   5/8"   7/8"

3 1/4"   1"

(A) Tenons may have to be cut down so they do not hit when inserted in post

2 3/4"

2 1/2"   5 15/16"

Turn waste tenon this size to turn taper,

Then turn to this size when ready for dovetails

7/8"

2"

2"

Head Stock End

CTRS-2

Tapered Section

1 1/4"

3/4"

1 1/8"

5/8"

1 grid square = 1"

Dovetail

For these three steps, see the PTRS-4 pattern on page 17. Complete the same processes, using the dimensions shown here.

Step 3: Set dovetail bit to full depth and rout in one pass

Step 2: Rout 1/2"-wide x 5/8"-deep dado in all three flats

120°

1 3/16"

Step 1: Rout flats

Shaker Pegs

by Robert Sonday

Note: It is best, if making several pegs at a time, to do each step to all pegs at a time. Although time is lost in putting the workpiece on and off the lathe several times, dimensional consistency among the pegs is gained.

Using the SPRS pattern Step 1 at right, put a peg blank between centers on the lathe, and turn it to a rough ¹⁵⁄₁₆"-diameter cylinder. Turn the tenon to ⅝" diameter x 1" long.

Using Step 2 at right, turn it to its finial-like shape, except for the cap end. Finish-sand it. After turning the first peg, use the profile gauge to hold the pattern for the rest of the pegs.

Using Step 3 at right, turn off the cap end.

Using Step 4 at right, sand the cap end grain on a foam covered disc with sandpaper applied to it. Hold the disc in a Jacob's chuck on the lathe and move the peg by hand, rotating it to finish the cap.

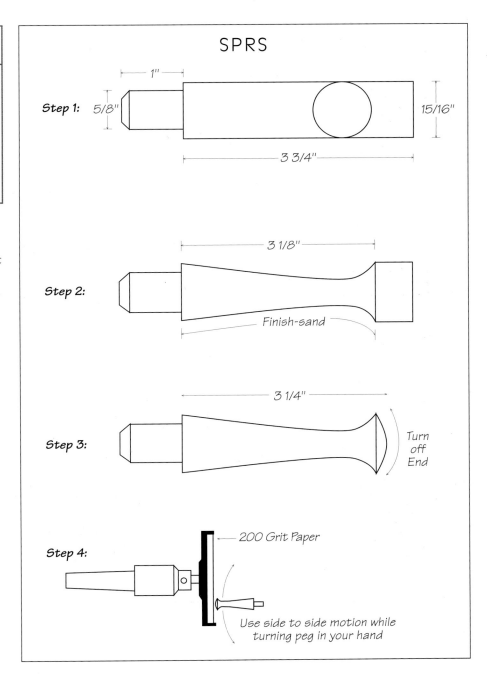

SPRS

Step 1: 1" — 5/8" — 15/16" — 3 3/4"

Step 2: 3 1/8" — Finish-sand

Step 3: 3 1/4" — Turn off End

Step 4: 200 Grit Paper — Use side to side motion while turning peg in your hand

Seating Series by Robert Sonday

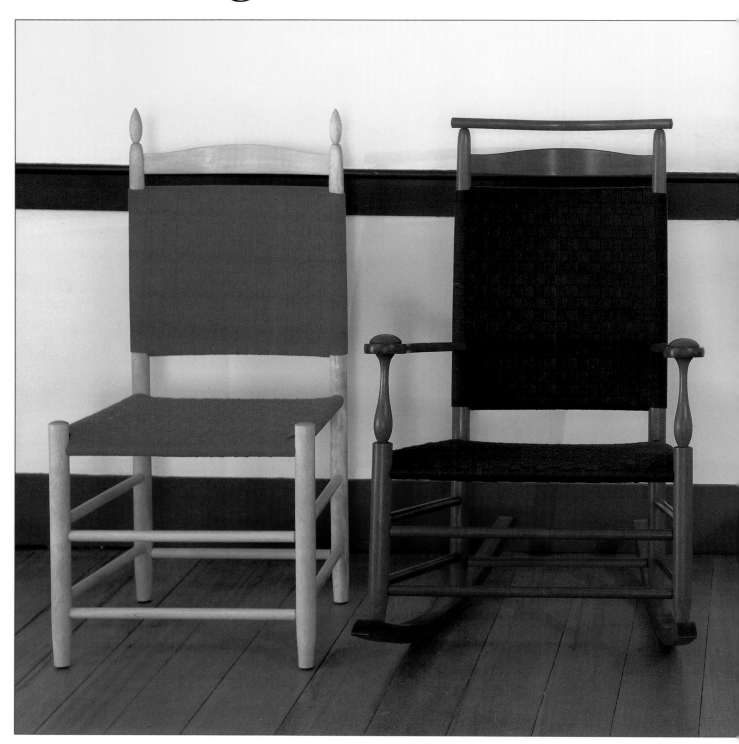

Have a seat. From left are Side Chair—Woven Back with Finials (instructions on page 49), Rocking Chair—Woven Back with Shawl Rail (instructions on page 62), Side Chair—Ladder Back with Finials (instructions on page 26), and Side Chair—Ladder Back with Shawl Rail (instructions on page 45).

Side Chair

—Ladder Back with Finials

FRONT POSTS A

Using the SSRS-1A pattern at right and the SSRS-2A pattern on opposite page, make two front posts, by first turning the stock from the 1⅝" square, to 1½" cylinders. Then turn them to finish shape, leaving the bottoms of the posts with no waste stock. Finish-sand the posts and turn them off to finished length. Turn a ³⁄₁₆" high dome at the top of the posts.

BACK POSTS A

Refer to SSRS-3A1 pattern on opposite page and the SSRS-3A pattern on page 28. For back posts, the directions are the same, except keep waste stock attached at the top ends of the posts after turning to shape, so they can be held while mortising and drilling later. At 20" from their bottom ends, begin a straight taper to 1" diameter at the top of the posts.

SANDING & DRILLING THE POSTS A

Finish-sand front and back posts. Then drill the stretcher holes for front and back stretchers, on the inside of each post on the drill press. Use a V-block to center the post under the bit.

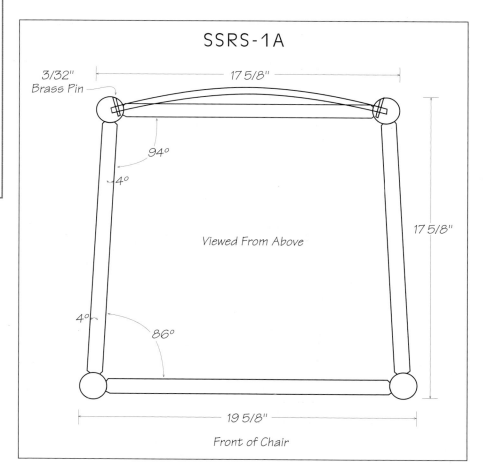

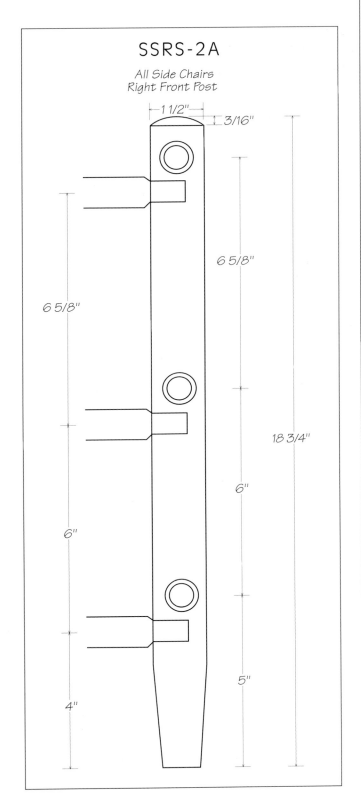

SSRS-2A

*All Side Chairs
Right Front Post*

1 1/2"
3/16"
6 5/8"
6 5/8"
18 3/4"
6"
6"
5"
4"

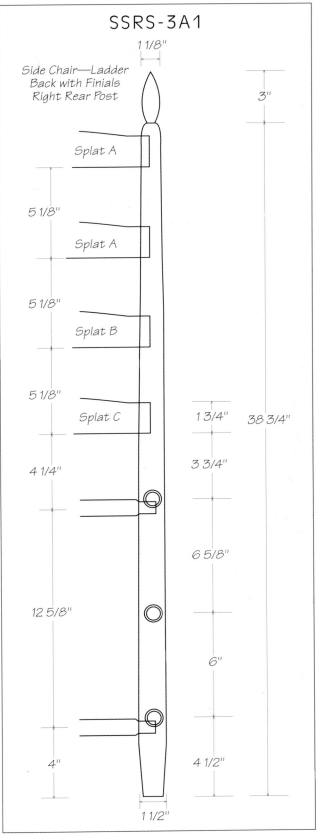

SSRS-3A1

*Side Chair—Ladder
Back with Finials
Right Rear Post*

1 1/8"
3"

Splat A
5 1/8"
Splat A
5 1/8"
Splat B
5 1/8"
Splat C
1 3/4"
38 3/4"
4 1/4"
3 3/4"
6 5/8"
12 5/8"
6"
4"
4 1/2"
1 1/2"

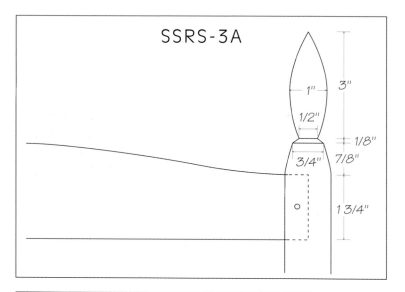

SSRS-3A

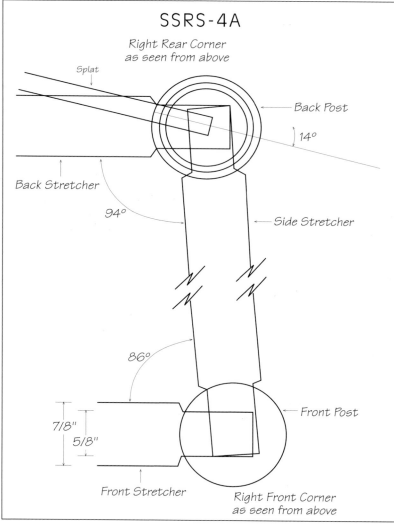

SSRS-4A

Right Rear Corner
as seen from above

Splat

Back Post

14°

Back Stretcher

94°

Side Stretcher

86°

7/8"
5/8"

Front Post

Front Stretcher

Right Front Corner
as seen from above

SPLAT MORTISES A

Make the splat mortises about 14° from the back plane of the chair. Put a mortising box on the lathe—see the guidelines for Mortising Box on page 11. Rout out the mortises. The mortises bottom out at the center of the post which, at maximum thickness, will be ¾" deep. All splats are the same length, as shown in the pattern SSRS-7 on page 30, to reach this center point of the post. Part off the post waste stock after all stretcher holes are drilled and splat mortises are routed. Use a rubber backed disc sander to sand the front post tops.

STRETCHERS A

Refer to the SSRS-4A pattern at left. Turn the stretchers to ⅞" diameter. Then turn the 1"-long tenons, ⅝" in diameter. Finish-sand the stretchers, but not the seat stretchers. Then crimp the tenons around their diameter with channel lock pliers, so they will expand in the joint, with glue, and not loosen over time.

SPLATS A

Follow these directions for making all splats—curves A, B & C. Make a form for each, following the different patterns in SSRS-6A–C on the opposite page.

Band-saw ⅛" x 2⅞" x 18" plies from the 1¾" x 2⅞" x 18" splat stock. Then abrasive-plane the plies down to the $^{33}/_{128}$" x 2⅞" x 18" splat ply thickness, which is $^{1}/_{128}$" over $^{1}/_{16}$". This makes the splats glue up to $^{17}/_{64}$" thick, which is $^{1}/_{64}$" over ¼". This extra thickness is for sanding down later to a perfect fit into the mortise. Match all splats in a set of chairs from the same, or matching boards.

To make the splat form, draw the splat's curve on the plywood pieces, as in the SSRS-5 pattern on the opposite page and the SSRS-6 pattern on page 30. Make certain to draw the full ¼" splat thickness on the form before band-sawing it to shape. The two form faces will have slightly different cut lines, to allow for the thickness of the splat, and to ensure a tight fit when clamping the splat glue-up. Cut out the

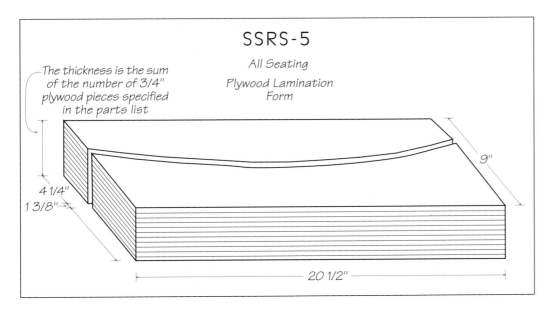

SSRS-5

All Seating

Plywood Lamination Form

The thickness is the sum of the number of 3/4" plywood pieces specified in the parts list

4 1/4"

1 3/8"

9"

20 1/2"

Shaker furniture appears simple, Shaker laws required that it be useful.

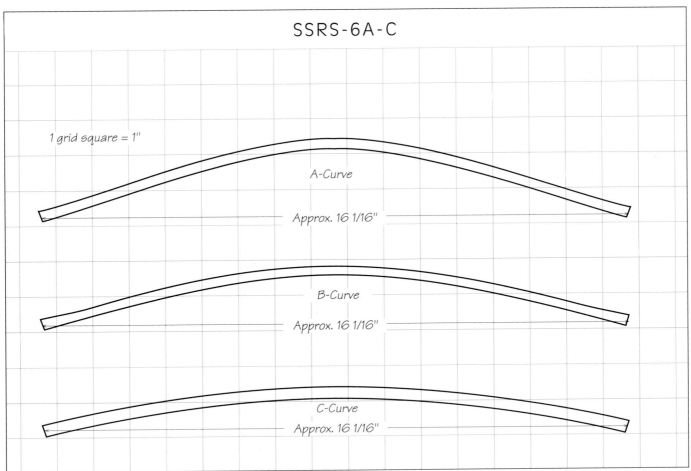

SSRS-6A-C

1 grid square = 1"

A-Curve

Approx. 16 1/16"

B-Curve

Approx. 16 1/16"

C-Curve

Approx. 16 1/16"

plywood pieces according to the cut lines, and then rout them. Stack-glue and screw them together, following the Form Making guidelines on page 11.

Refer to the SSRS-7 pattern at right. To glue up the splat, spread glue on all mating surfaces of the four plies and then stack them. Then put them in between the mating form surfaces, close the form together, and clamp the form shut tightly until the glue cures.

Then unclamp and remove the splat. After all the splats are glued up, cut them to finish length. Then draw the splats' front elevation on the faces of the splats. Cut off the excess with the band saw. Knock the corners off the top and bottom edges of the splats by rough sanding.

Using SSRS-7A pattern on opposite page, make a scraping tool by grinding a ⅛" radius semi-circle into a flexible scraper blade for rounding out the splat edges further.

Scrape the top and bottom splat edges down to a ⅛" radius with the scraper, and then finish-sand those edges. Fit each splat to its particular mortises by hand-sanding the splat faces and/or top or bottom edges. Finish-sand the splats.

FRONT ASSEMBLY A
Parts are now all machined and finished, but not yet drilled for the side stretcher holes. Assemble the front section with glue: two front posts and the three stretchers that span between them. One clamp on each spanning member should be sufficient. Make certain the assembly stays in its flat, symmetrical plane by twisting out any unevenness before leaving it to set up.

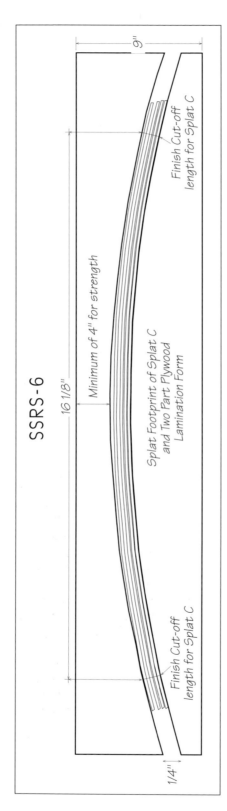

SSRS-6

9"

16 1/8"

Minimum of 4" for strength

Finish Cut-off length for Splat C

Splat Footprint of Splat C and Two Part Plywood Lamination Form

Finish Cut-off length for Splat C

1/4"

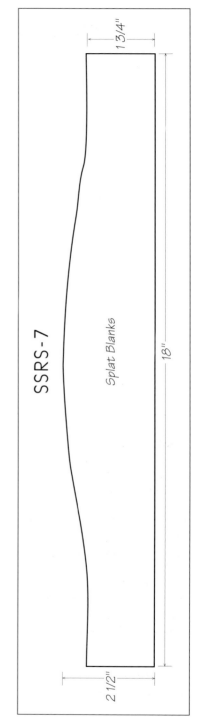

SSRS-7

1 3/4"

18"

Splat Blanks

2 1/2"

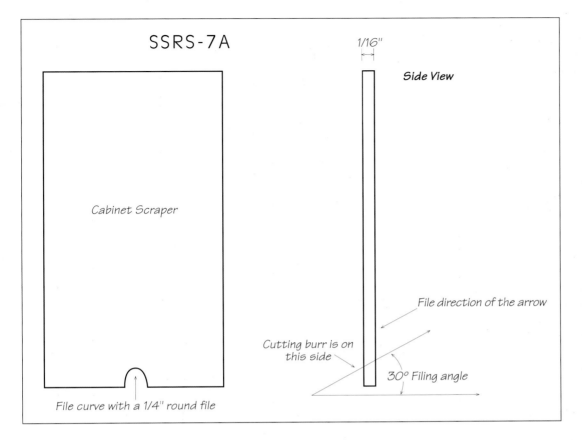

SSRS-7A

Cabinet Scraper

File curve with a 1/4" round file

1/16"

Side View

File direction of the arrow

Cutting burr is on this side

30° Filing angle

Purity, simplicity, honesty, utility, order, and economy should be reflected in their souls and in their dwellings.

BACK ASSEMBLY A

Assemble the back section: the two tall posts, with the two stretchers and four splats that span them. Again, make certain the assembly stays in its flat, symmetrical plane by twisting out any unevenness before leaving it to set up. When it is dry, pin the top slat tenons with the ³⁄₃₂" brass pin from the back by drilling a hole and epoxying in a piece of rod. Cut the rod and file it flush. Refer to SSRS-1A pattern on page 26.

FULL ASSEMBLY A

With the glue of both assemblies cured, they are ready for drilling side stretcher holes on the drill press about 4° off of square as seen from above, so the seat tapers larger to its front. Stretchers are all perpendicular to the upright posts, as seen from the chair sides, front and rear. A ½" tilt for comfort is accomplished now through the ½" discrepancy between the front and back post stretcher hole heights off the floor. The holes now being drilled for the side stretchers drill into the rear stretcher tenons. This is traditional for chairs. Then, in one assembly, glue all six side stretchers into the front section, just before gluing them into the back assembly. Again, rack the chair to correct for any unevenness after gluing and clamping if all four legs don't touch the flat table saw surface at once.

FINISH A

After the glue cures, apply two coats of oil and then one coat of wax.

WEAVING

When finish has cured, follow instructions on page 66 for Seat Weaving—Side Chair.

Sitting pretty. An end view of six ash Side Chairs—Ladder Back with Finials at the ash Trestle Table (instructions on page 73).

Arm Chair
—Ladder Back with Finials

FRONT POSTS B

Using the SSRS-1D pattern at right, the SSRS-2B pattern on page 34, make two front posts, by first drilling a hole ½" diameter x ¾" deep in the top ends. Lathe-turn the stock from the 1⅝" square, to a 1½" cylinder. Then turn them to finish shape. Make an adapter with a ½" o.d. tenon to fit the live center on the lathe.

BACK POSTS B

Refer to the SSRS-3A4 pattern on page 34 and the SSRS-3A pattern on page 35. For the back posts, first lathe-turn the stock from 1⅝" square, to 1½" cylinders. Then turn them to finish shape, leaving the bottoms of the posts with no waste stock. Keep waste stock attached at the top ends of the posts after turning to shape, so they can be held while drilling and mortising later. At 20" from their bottom ends, begin a straight taper down to 1" diameter at the top of the posts.

SANDING & DRILLING THE POSTS A

Finish-sand front and back posts. Then drill the stretcher holes for front and back stretchers on the inside of each post on the drill press. Use a V-block to center the post under the bit.

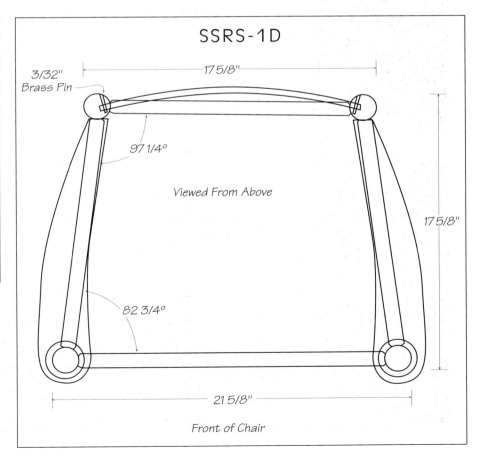

SSRS-1D

3/32" Brass Pin

17 5/8"

97 1/4°

Viewed From Above

17 5/8"

82 3/4°

21 5/8"

Front of Chair

SSRS-2B

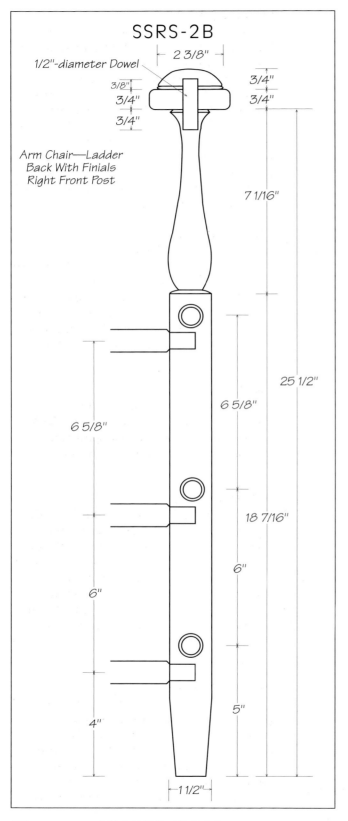

1/2"-diameter Dowel

2 3/8"

3/8"
3/4"
3/4"

3/4"
3/4"

Arm Chair—Ladder
Back With Finials
Right Front Post

7 1/16"

25 1/2"

6 5/8"

6 5/8"

18 7/16"

6 5/8"

6"

6"

4"

5"

1 1/2"

SSRS-3A4

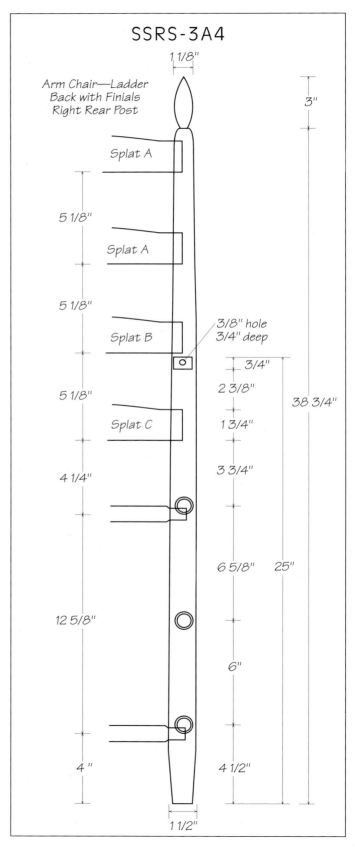

1 1/8"

Arm Chair—Ladder
Back with Finials
Right Rear Post

3"

Splat A

Splat A

5 1/8"

5 1/8"

Splat B

3/8" hole
3/4" deep

5 1/8"

3/4"

2 3/8"

Splat C

1 3/4"

4 1/4"

3 3/4"

38 3/4"

6 5/8"

25"

12 5/8"

6"

4 "

4 1/2"

1 1/2"

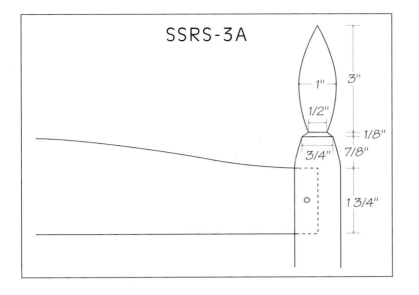

SSRS-3A

1" · 3"

1/2"

1/8"

3/4" · 7/8"

1 3/4"

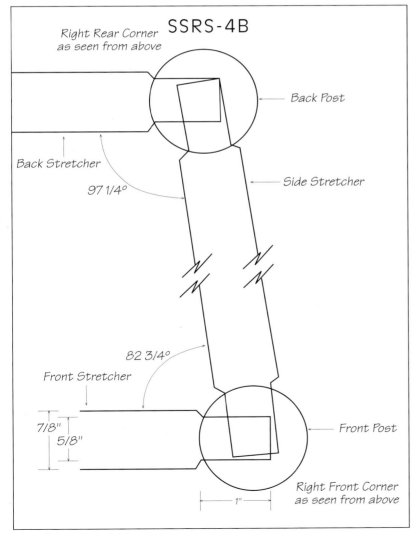

SSRS-4B

Right Rear Corner
as seen from above

Back Post

Back Stretcher

97 1/4°

Side Stretcher

82 3/4°

Front Stretcher

7/8"
5/8"

Front Post

Right Front Corner
as seen from above

1"

SPLAT MORTISES B

Make the splat mortises about 14° from the back plane of the chair. Put a mortising box on the lathe—see the guidelines for the Mortising Box on page 11. Rout out the mortises. The mortises bottom out at the center of the post which, at maximum thickness, will be ¾" deep. All splats are the same length, as shown in the SSRS-7 pattern on page 30, to reach this center point of the post. Part off the post waste stock after all stretcher holes are drilled and splat mortises are routed.

STRETCHERS A

Referring to the SSRS-4B pattern at left, turn the stretchers to ⅞" diameter. Then turn the 1"-long tenons, ⅝" in diameter. Finish-sand the stretchers, but not the seat stretchers. Then crimp the tenons around their diameter with channel lock pliers, so they will expand in the joint, with glue, and not loosen over time.

SPLATS A

Make the splats according to the instructions for Side Chair—Ladder Back with Finials on page 28, using the same splat drawings as in SSRS-6A–C on page 29.

FRONT ASSEMBLY A

Parts are now all machined and finished, but not yet drilled for the side stretcher holes. Assemble the front section with glue: two front posts and the three stretchers that span between them. One clamp on each spanning member should be sufficient. Make certain the assembly stays in its flat, symmetrical plane by twisting out any unevenness before leaving it to set up.

BACK ASSEMBLY A

Assemble the back section: the two tall posts, with the two stretchers and four splats that span them. Again, make certain the assembly stays in its flat, symmetrical plane by twisting out any unevenness before leaving it to set up. When it is dry, pin the top slat tenons with the 3⁄32" brass pin from the back by drilling a hole and epoxying in a piece of rod. Cut the rod and file it flush.

ARM SLOTS A
Refer to SSRS-3A4 pattern on page 34. To make slots for the arms, clamp a ¾" x 26" x 40" wood straightedge across the back assembly, perpendicular to the posts, next to the arm slot location. Then rout the slots with a top bearing ¾" diameter straight-face bit, guiding the bearing against the straight-edge. Set the bit to cut the dado ³⁄₁₆" deep.

Note: The straightedge must be clamped to the bottom of the chair frame so it runs off of the 1½"-diameter straight section of the post and cantilevers out over the tapered section of the post, where slots are to be cut.

FULL ASSEMBLY A
With the glue of both assemblies cured, drill the side stretcher holes on the drill press about 7¼° off square as seen from above, so the seat tapers larger to its front. Stretchers are all perpendicular to

the upright posts, as seen from the chair sides, front and rear. A ½" tilt for comfort is accomplished now through the ½" discrepancy between the front and back post stretcher hole heights off the floor. The holes now being drilled for the side stretchers are drilled into the rear stretcher tenons. This is traditional for chairs. Then, in one assembly, glue in all six side stretchers into the front section, just before gluing them into the back assembly. Again, rack the chair to correct any unevenness, after gluing and clamping, if all four legs don't touch the flat table saw surface at once.

ARMS A
Using SSRS-8A pattern below, draw the outline of the arms on the arm blanks, and then band-saw them to shape. Sand their edge profiles to shape. Test-fit the arms to the slots in the back posts. Drill the ½" hole in the arms for the dowel. Drill the ⅜" hole into the back posts, and into the back ends of the arms. Finish-sand the arms.

When doing the first glue-up to

install the arms, don't glue the front joint at the front posts. Put a dry, unglued 2" dowel in the joint to register it with the front post top. Then glue the rear joint in the back post slots, using the 1½" long, ⅜" dowel. Clamp the joint tight.

Drill the ½" diameter hole, ⅜" deep into the center of the pommel stock. Band-saw each stock piece to a disc. Turn them to their profile, and then turn the small bead at their circumference. Finish-sand them.

Now assemble the front post top joint with glue, with the front of the arm and pommel. Use the dry registration dowel from the previous glue-up. Clamp this joint tightly.

FINISH A
After the glue cures, apply two coats of oil and then one coat of wax.

WEAVING
When finish has cured, follow instructions on page 67 for Seat Weaving—Arm Chair.

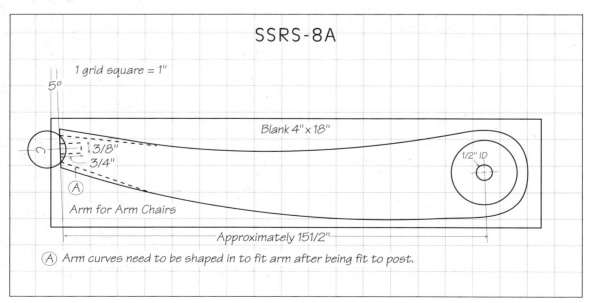

SSRS-8A

1 grid square = 1"

5°

Blank 4" x 18"

3/8"
3/4"

1/2" ID

Ⓐ

Arm for Arm Chairs

Approximately 15 1/2"

Ⓐ Arm curves need to be shaped in to fit arm after being fit to post.

Resting place. Curly maple Arm Chair—Ladder Back with Finials
gives a place to the wooden hat made by Johannes Michelsen.

Soothing rockers. Left to right are the Rocking Chair—Ladder Back with Finials, the Pedestal Table (instructions on page 15), the Hog Scraper Candlestick (instructions on page 85), and the Rocking Chair—Woven Back with Shawl Rail (instructions on page 62).

Rocking Chair

—Ladder Back with Finials

SPECIFICATIONS

BASICS
Material: bird's eye maple
Overall Dimensions: 42" high x 25¼" wide x 33" dia.
Finish: oil and wax

PART LIST

Bird's eye maple		
Back posts	(2)	1⅝" x 1⅝" x 42½"
Front posts	(2)	1⅝" x 1⅝" x 20½"
Front stretchers	(2)	15/16" x 15/16" x 22⅝"
Side stretchers	(4)	15/16" x 15/16" x 17⅝"
Rear stretcher	(1)	15/16" x 15/16" x 16⅝"
Splat stock	(4)	1¾" x 2⅞" x 18"
Arms	(2)	¾" x 4" wide x 19" long
Pommels	(2)	¾" x 2⅝" square
Rocker stock	(2)	1⅝" x 3" x 36"
Hickory		
Front seat stretcher	(1)	15/16" x 15/16" x 22⅝"
Side stretchers	(2)	15/16" x 15/16" x 17⅝"
Rear stretchers	(1)	15/16" x 15/16" x 16⅝"
Plywood		
Splat form layers	(12)	¾" x 9" x 20½" (four for each curve A, B, & C)
Rocker form layers	(3)	¾" x 15" x 36"
Dowels		
Arm back	(2)	⅜" x 1½"
Front	(2)	½" x 1 13/16"
Rockers	(4)	½" x 2"

SSRS-1E

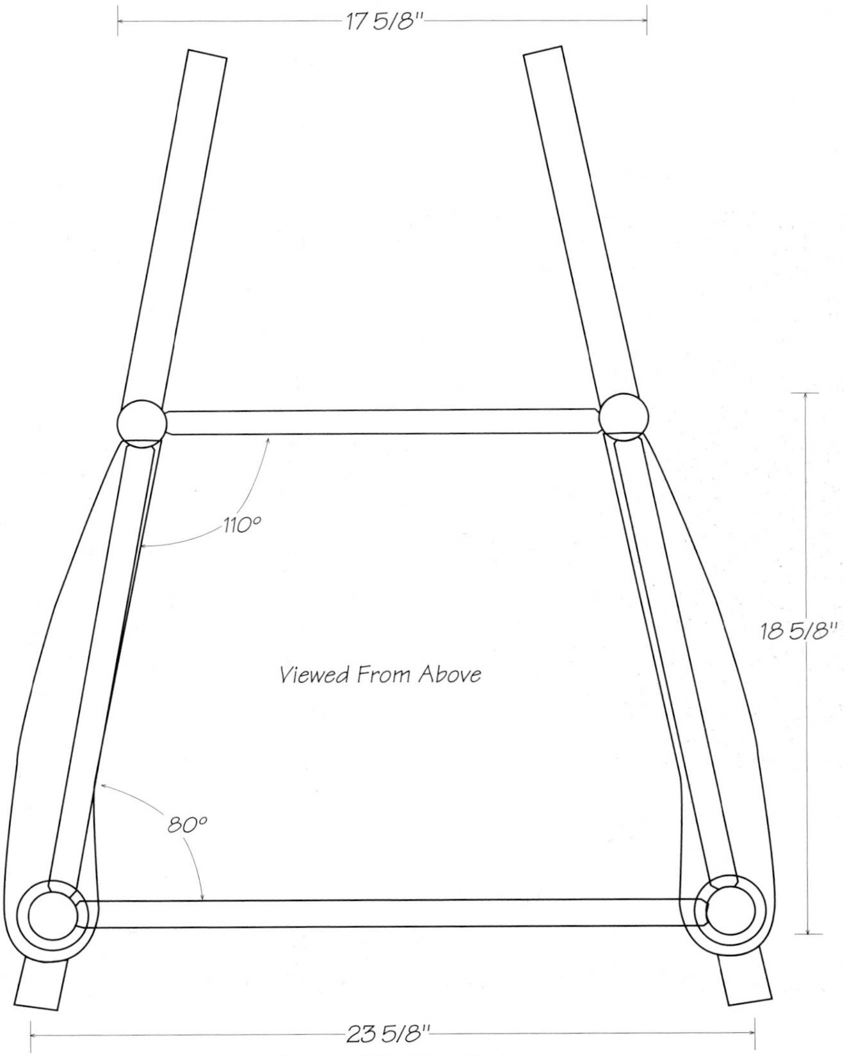

17 5/8"
110°
18 5/8"
Viewed From Above
80°
23 5/8"

Front of Rocking Chair

They lifted their hands to work and their hearts to God.

SSRS-2C

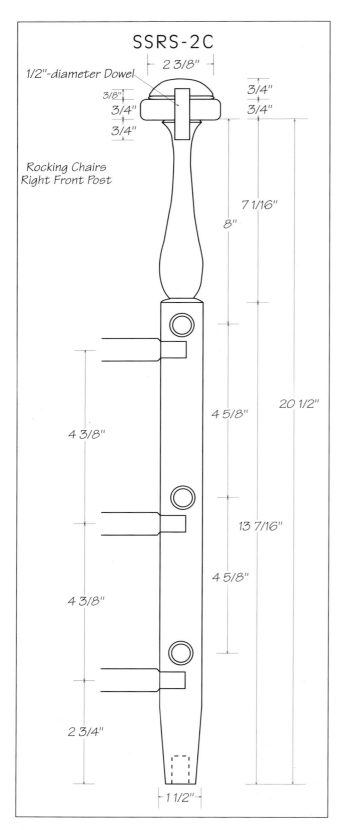

1/2"-diameter Dowel

3/8"
3/4"
3/4"

2 3/8"

3/4"
3/4"
3/4"

Rocking Chairs
Right Front Post

7 1/16"

8"

20 1/2"

4 5/8"

4 3/8"

13 7/16"

4 5/8"

4 3/8"

2 3/4"

1 1/2"

SSRS-3A5

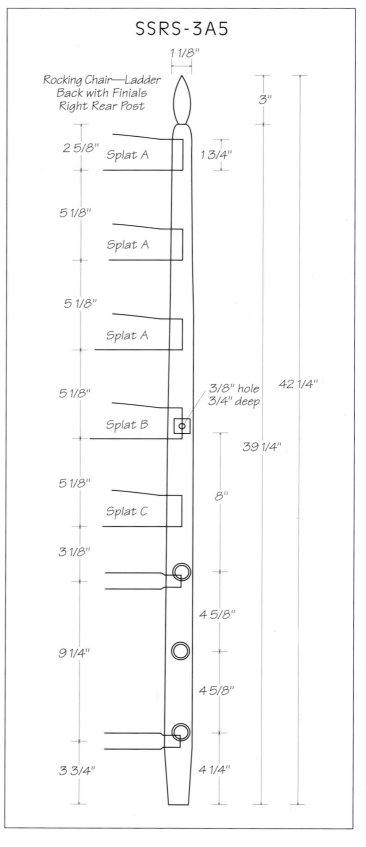

1 1/8"

Rocking Chair—Ladder
Back with Finials
Right Rear Post

3"

2 5/8"   Splat A   1 3/4"

5 1/8"   Splat A

5 1/8"   Splat A

42 1/4"

5 1/8"   Splat B   3/8" hole
3/4" deep

39 1/4"

5 1/8"   Splat C   8"

3 1/8"

4 5/8"

9 1/4"

4 5/8"

3 3/4"   4 1/4"

FRONT POSTS C

Using the SSRS-1E pattern on page 39 and the SSRS-2C pattern on the opposite page, make two front posts, by first drilling a hole ½" diameter x ¾" deep in the top ends. Then drill a hole ½" diameter x 1⅜" deep in the bottom ends. Lathe-turn the stock from the 1⅝" square, to 1½" cylinders. Then turn them to finish shape. Don't make any cuts now on the bottom ends—leave them long.

Make a drive center with a ½"-o.d. tenon to drive the posts and also a 1½"-o.d. adapter for the live center.

BACK POSTS C

Refer to the SSRS-3A5 pattern on the opposite page and the SSRS-3A at right. For the back posts, first drill a hole in the bottom ends, ½" diameter, 2¼" long. Then lathe-turn the stock from 1⅝" square, to a 1½" cylinder. At 20" from their bottom ends, begin a straight taper down to 1" diameter at the top of the posts. Then turn them to finish shape, leaving the bottoms of the posts long—wait until the end of the project to cut them to receive the rockers. Keep waste stock attached at the top ends of the posts after turning to shape, so they can be held while drilling and mortising later.

SANDING & DRILLING THE POSTS A

Finish-sand front and back posts. Then drill the stretcher holes for front and back stretchers, on the inside of each post on the drill press.

SPLAT MORTISES B

Make the splat mortises about 14° from the back plane of the chair. Put a router box on the lathe—see the guidelines for the Mortising Box on page 11. Rout out the mortises. The mortises bottom out at the

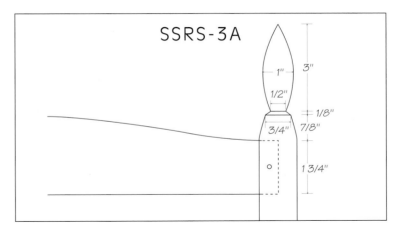

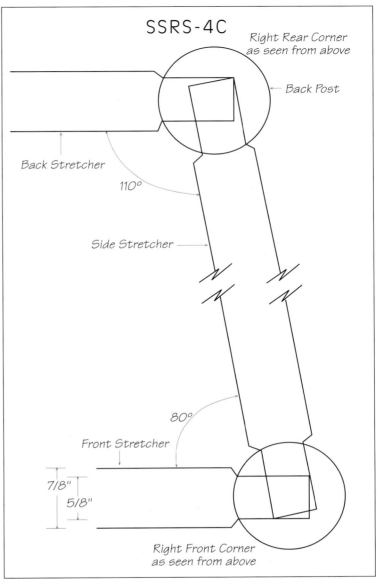

center of the posts which, at maximum thickness, will be ¾" deep. All splats are the same length, to reach this center point of the posts. Part off the post waste stock after all stretcher holes are drilled and splat mortises are routed.

STRETCHERS A
Using the SSRS-4C pattern on page 41, turn the stretchers to ⅞" diameter. Then turn the 1" long tenons, ⅝" in diameter. Finish-sand the stretchers, but not the seat stretchers. Crimp the tenons around their diameter with channel lock pliers, so they will expand in the joint, with glue, and not loosen over time.

SPLATS A
Make the splats according to the instructions for Side Chair—Ladder Back with Finials on page 28, using the same drawings in SSRS-6A–C patterns on page 29.

FRONT ASSEMBLY A
Parts are now all machined and finished, but not yet drilled for the side stretcher holes. Assemble the front section with glue: two front

posts and the three stretchers that span between them. One clamp on each spanning member should be sufficient. Make certain the assembly stays in its flat, symmetrical plane by twisting out any unevenness before leaving it to set up.

BACK ASSEMBLY A
Assemble the back section: the two tall posts, with the two stretchers and four splats that span them. Again, make certain the assembly stays in its flat, symmetrical plane by twisting out any unevenness before leaving it to set up. When dry, pin the top slat tenons with the ³⁄₃₂" brass pin from the back by drilling a hole and epoxying in a piece of rod. Cut the rod and file it flush.

ARM SLOTS A
Refer to SSRS-3A5 pattern on page 40. To make slots for the arms, clamp a ¾" x 26" x 40" wood straightedge across the back assembly, perpendicular to the post, next to the arm slot location. Then rout the slots with a top bearing ¾" diameter straight-face bit, guiding

the bearing against the straight-edge. Set the bit to cut the dado ³⁄₁₆" deep.

Note: The straightedge must be clamped to the bottom of the chair frame so it runs off of the 1½"-diameter straight section of the post and cantilevers out over the tapered section of the post, where slots are to be cut.

FULL ASSEMBLY A
With the glue of both assemblies cured, they are ready for drilling side stretcher holes on the drill press about 10° off square as seen from above, so the seat tapers larger to its front. Stretchers are all perpendicular to the upright posts, as seen from the chair sides, front and rear. Lay out side stretchers using patterns SSRS-2C and SSRS-3A5 on page 40. The holes now being drilled for the side stretchers are drilled into the rear stretcher tenons. This is traditional for chairs. Then, in one assembly, glue in all six side stretchers into the front section, just before gluing them into the back assembly. Again, rack the chair to correct any unevenness,

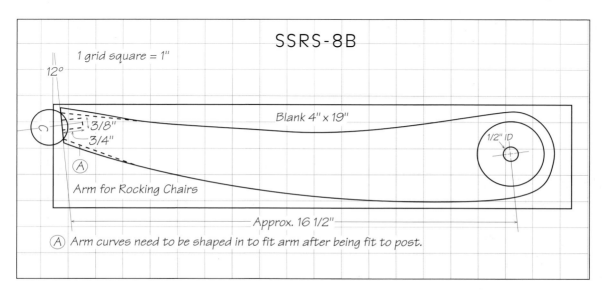

SSRS-8B

1 grid square = 1"

12°

3/8"
3/4"

Blank 4" x 19"

1/2" ID

Ⓐ

Arm for Rocking Chairs

Approx. 16 1/2"

Ⓐ Arm curves need to be shaped in to fit arm after being fit to post.

after gluing and clamping, if all four legs don't touch the flat table saw surface at once.

ARMS

Make the arms according to the instructions for Arm Chair—Ladder Back with Finial on page 36, except use the drawing SSRS-8B.

ROCKERS A

Refer to pattern SSRS-9 at right. Band-saw ³⁄₁₆" x 1⅝" x 36" plies from the rocker stock. Then abrasive-plane the plies down to the ⅛" x 1⅝" x 36" rocker ply thickness. This makes the rockers glue up to 1⅜" thick. Keep all the plies in the order they came from the stock, so the grain matches well.

To make the form for the rockers, draw the rocker's curve on the plywood pieces, as in the form drawing SSRS-10 on page 44. Make certain to draw the full 1⅜" splat thickness on the form before band-sawing it to shape. The two form faces will have slightly different cut lines, to allow for the thickness of the rocker, to ensure a tight fit when clamping the rocker glue-up. Cut out the plywood pieces according to the cut lines, and then rout them. Stack-glue and screw them, following the Form Making guidelines on page 11. Also refer to drawing SSRS-6 on page 30.

Shaker Words:

Do all the good you can
In all the ways you can
To all the people you can
In every place you can
At all the times you can
As long as you ever can

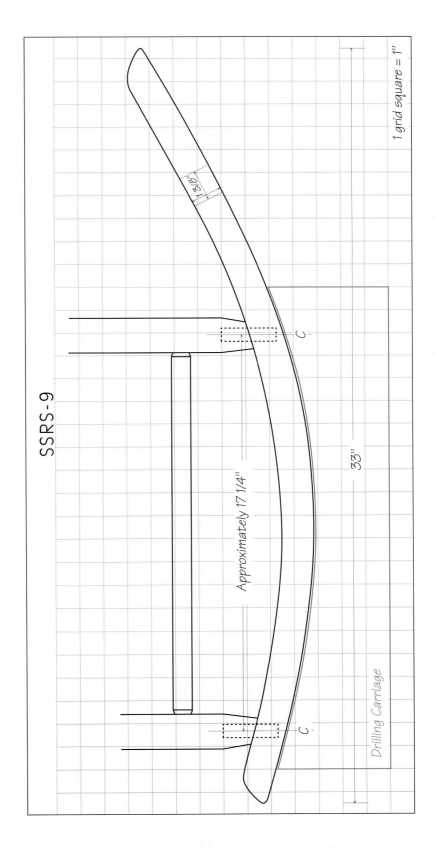

SSRS-9

1 grid square = 1"

1⅜"

Approximately 17 1/4"

33"

Drilling Carriage

C

C

Cope-cut the bottoms of the posts to fit the curve of the rocker. Also, make up a drilling carriage to hold rockers in while drilling for dowel holes.

To glue up a rocker, spread glue on all mating surfaces of the 11 plies, and then stack them. Put them in between the mating form surfaces, close the form together, and clamp the form shut tightly until the glue cures.

Unclamp and remove the rocker. After each rocker glue-up is done,

clean the dried glue off the edges. True them by joining one edge, and then planing the other to achieve 1⅜" thickness. Band-saw to finish-shape on both ends. Finish-sand them.

Cut off the post bottoms to the angles of the rockers, fitting more exactly to the rockers' profile after the initial cuts. Test that the chair rocks evenly front to back, on the rockers while removing high points successively. Mark the rocker hole centers by inserting dowel centers in the post bottom holes, and

pressing the rockers onto the points of the dowel centers. Drill holes in the rockers, and then epoxy the rockers to the chair, with the dowels.

FINISH A
After the glue cures, apply two coats of oil and then one coat of wax.

WEAVING
When finish has cured, follow instructions on page 68 for Seat Weaving—Rocking Chair.

To the Shaker, work was worship, and all worked to improve their time and talents in life, in that manner in which they might be most useful.

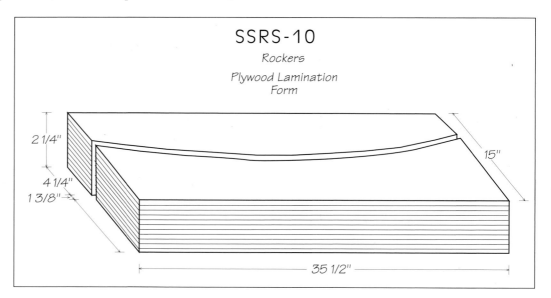

SSRS-10

Rockers

Plywood Lamination Form

2 1/4"

4 1/4"

1 3/8"

15"

35 1/2"

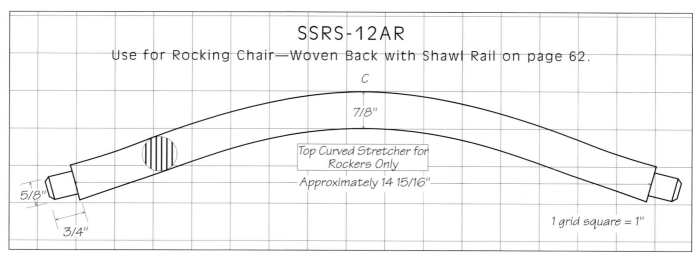

SSRS-12AR

Use for Rocking Chair—Woven Back with Shawl Rail on page 62.

C

7/8"

Top Curved Stretcher for Rockers Only

Approximately 14 15/16"

5/8"

3/4"

1 grid square = 1"

Side Chair
—Ladder Back with Shawl Rail

FRONT POSTS A
Using the SSRS-1B pattern at right and the SSRS-2A pattern on page 46, make two front posts, by first turning the stock from the 1⅝" square, to 1½" cylinders. Then turn them to finish shape, leaving the bottoms of the posts with no waste stock. Finish-sand the posts and turn them off to finished length. Turn a ³⁄₁₆" high dome at the tops of the posts.

BACK POSTS D
Refer to the SSRS-3A2 pattern on page 46 and the SSRS-3B on page 47. For back posts, the directions are the same, except keep waste stock attached at the top ends of the posts after turning to shape, so they can be held while mortising and drilling later. At 20" from their bottom ends, begin a straight taper to 1" diameter at the tops of the posts.

SANDING & DRILLING THE POSTS A
Finish-sand front and back posts. Then drill the stretcher holes for front and back stretchers, on the inside of each post on the drill press. Use a V-block to center the post under the bit.

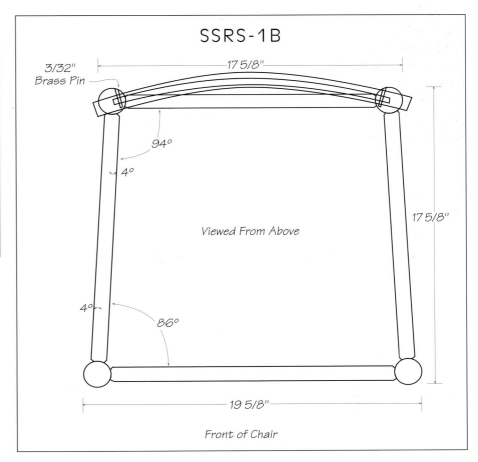

SSRS-1B

3/32" Brass Pin

17 5/8"

94°

4°

Viewed From Above

17 5/8"

4°

86°

19 5/8"

Front of Chair

SSRS-2A

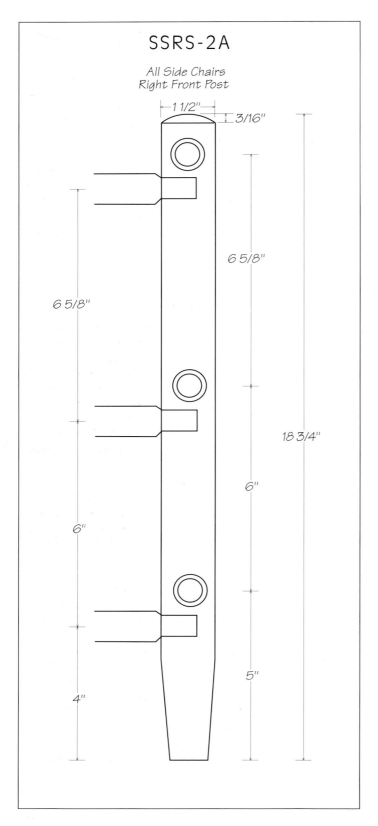

All Side Chairs
Right Front Post

1 1/2"
3/16"
6 5/8"
6 5/8"
18 3/4"
6"
6"
5"
4"

SSRS-3A2

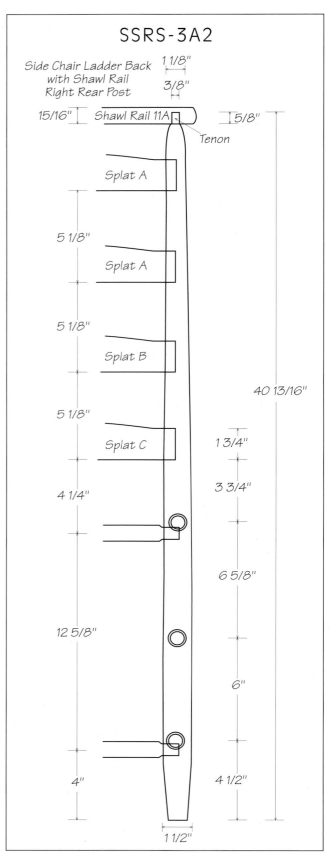

Side Chair Ladder Back
with Shawl Rail
Right Rear Post

1 1/8"
3/8"
15/16"   Shawl Rail 11A   5/8"
Tenon

Splat A

5 1/8"

Splat A

5 1/8"

Splat B

5 1/8"

Splat C

4 1/4"

40 13/16"

1 3/4"

3 3/4"

6 5/8"

12 5/8"

6"

4"

4 1/2"

1 1/2"

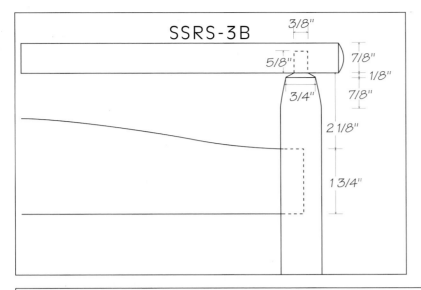

SSRS-3B

3/8"
5/8" 7/8"
1/8"
3/4" 7/8"
2 1/8"
1 3/4"

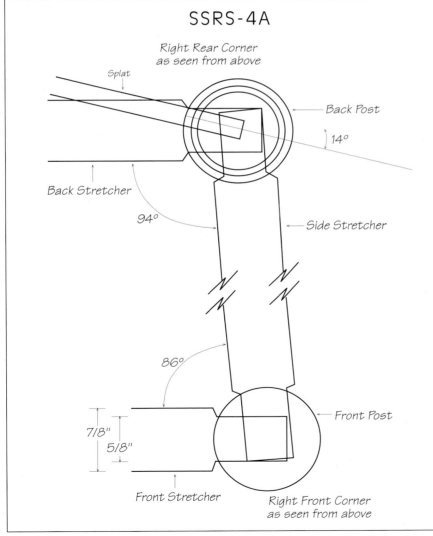

SSRS-4A

Right Rear Corner
as seen from above

Splat

Back Post

14°

Back Stretcher

94°

Side Stretcher

86°

Front Post

7/8"
5/8"

Front Stretcher

Right Front Corner
as seen from above

SPLAT MORTISES A

Make the splat mortises about 14° from the back plane of the chair. Put a router box on the lathe—see the guidelines for the Mortising Box on page 11. Rout out the mortises. The mortises bottom out at the center of the post which, at maximum thickness, will be ¾" deep. All splats are the same length, as shown in pattern SSRS-7 on page 30, to reach this center point of the post. Part off the post waste stock after all stretcher holes are drilled and splat mortises are routed. Use a rubber backed disc sander to sand the front post tops.

STRETCHERS A

Using the SSRS-4A pattern at left, turn the stretchers to ⅞" diameter. Then turn the 1"-long tenons, ⅝" in diameter. Finish-sand the stretchers, but not the seat stretchers. Then crimp the tenons around their diameter with channel lock pliers, so they will expand in the joint, with glue, and not loosen over time.

SPLATS A

Make the splats according to the instructions for Side Chair—Ladder Back with Finials on page 28, using the same drawings in SSRS-6A–C patterns on page 29.

FRONT ASSEMBLY A

Parts are now all machined and finished, but not yet drilled for the side stretcher holes. Assemble the front section with glue: two front posts and the three stretchers that span between them. One clamp on each spanning member should be sufficient. Make certain the assembly stays in its flat, symmetrical plane by twisting out any unevenness before leaving it to set up.

BACK ASSEMBLY A

Assemble the back section: the two tall posts, with the two stretchers and four splats that span them. Again, make certain the assembly stays in its flat, symmetrical plane by twisting out any unevenness before leaving it to set up. When dry, pin the top slat tenons with the ³⁄₃₂" brass pin from the back by drilling a hole and epoxying in a piece of rod. Cut the rod and file it flush. See the SSRS-1B pattern on page 45.

FULL ASSEMBLY A

With the glue of both assemblies cured, they are ready for drilling side stretcher holes on the drill press about 4° off of square as seen from above, so the seat tapers larger to its front. Stretchers are all perpendicular to the upright posts, as seen from the chair sides, front and rear. A ½" tilt for comfort is accomplished now through the ½" discrepancy between the front and back post stretcher hole heights off the floor. The holes now being drilled for the side stretchers are drilled into the rear stretcher tenons. This is traditional for chairs. Then, in one assembly, glue in all six side stretchers into the front section, just before gluing them into the back assembly. Again, rack the

chair to correct any unevenness, after gluing and clamping, if all four legs don't touch the flat table saw surface at once.

SHAWL RAIL A (SHALLOW CURVE)

Using the SSRS-11A pattern below, band-saw ⅛" x 1⅛" x 21½" plies from the shawl rail stock. Then abrasive-plane the plies down to the ¹⁄₁₆" x 1⅛" x 21½" shawl rail ply thickness. This makes the shawl rail glue up to ¹⁵⁄₁₆" thick with 15 plies. Keep them in the order they came from the stock, so the grain matches.

To make the shawl rail form, consult pattern SSRS-6 on page 30 to find the shawl rail, then draw the shawl rail's curve on the plywood pieces, as in the form drawing. Make certain to draw the full ¹⁵⁄₁₆" shawl rail thickness on the form before band-sawing it to shape. The two form faces will have slightly different cut lines, to allow for the thickness of the shawl rail, and to ensure a tight fit when clamping the shawl rail glue-up. Cut out the plywood pieces according to the cut lines, and then rout them. Stack-glue and screw them, following the Form Making guidelines on page 11. Refer also to pattern SSRS-5 on page 29.

To glue up the shawl rail, spread glue on all mating surfaces of the 15 plies, and then stack them. Put them in between the mating form surfaces, close the form together, and clamp the form shut tightly until the glue cures.

Unclamp and remove the shawl rail. Clean the dried glue off the edges, and then join one edge. Plane the opposite edge to achieve ¹⁵⁄₁₆" thickness. Then rout each corner off the shawl rail, making it circular in section. Finish-sand it.

Lay the shawl rail in place onto the tenons on the back post tops. Mark where the tenons indicate holes to be drilled in the underside of the shawl rail. Drill holes. Cut the shawl rail to finish length. Sand the ends to their slightly rounded profile, and then finish-sand them.

Glue the shawl rail onto the chair.

FINISH A

After the glue cures, apply two coats of oil and then one coat of wax.

WEAVING

When finish has cured, follow instructions on page 66 for Seat Weaving—Side Chair.

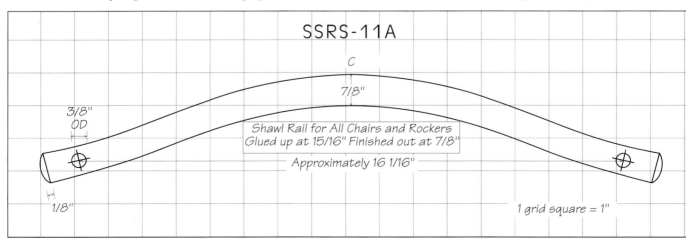

SSRS-11A

C

7/8"

3/8"
OD

Shawl Rail for All Chairs and Rockers
Glued up at 15/16" Finished out at 7/8"

Approximately 16 1/16"

1/8"

1 grid square = 1"

Side Chair
—Woven Back with Finials

SPECIFICATIONS

BASICS
Material: pao amarillo
  or yellow-dyed maple
Overall Dimensions: 41¾" high x
  19⅝" wide x 18⅛" dia.
Finish: oil and wax

PART LIST
Pao amarillo or yellow-dyed maple
Back posts (2)	1⅝" x 1⅝" x 42½"
Front posts (2)	1⅝" x 1⅝" x 19½"
Front stretchers (2)	¹⁵⁄₁₆" x ¹⁵⁄₁₆" x 18⅝"
Side & rear stretchers (5)	¹⁵⁄₁₆" x ¹⁵⁄₁₆" x 16⅝"
Splat stock (1)	1¾" x 2⅞" x 18"

Hickory
Front seat stretcher (1)	¹⁵⁄₁₆" x ¹⁵⁄₁₆" x 18⅝"
Side & rear stretchers (3)	¹⁵⁄₁₆" x ¹⁵⁄₁₆" x 16⅝"
Curved stretcher stock (1)	1⅛" x 2" x 21½"

Plywood
Splat form layers (4)	¾" x 9" x 20½"
Curved stretcher form layers (4)	¾" x 9" x 20½"
(two for each curve A & C)	

FRONT POSTS A

Using the SSRS-1C pattern at right and the SSRS-2A pattern on page 50, make two front posts, by first turning the stock from the 1⅝" square, to 1½" cylinders. Then turn them to finish shape, leaving the bottoms of the posts with no waste stock. Finish-sand the posts and turn them off to finished length. Turn a ³⁄₁₆" high dome at the top of the posts.

BACK POSTS A

Refer to pattern SSRS-3A3 on page 50 and pattern SSRS-3A on page 51. For back posts, the directions are the same, except keep waste stock attached at the top ends of the posts after turning to shape, so they can be held while mortising and drilling later. At 20" from their bottom ends, begin a straight taper to 1" diameter at the top of posts.

SANDING & DRILLING THE POSTS B

Finish-sand front and back posts. Then drill the stretcher holes for front and back stretchers, on the inside of each post on the drill press. The curved stretcher holes are at different angles to the back plane of the chair for each stretcher. Use a V-block to center the post under the bit.

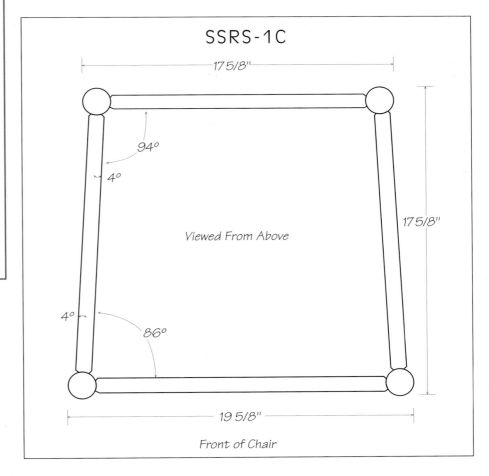

SSRS-1C

17 5/8"

94°

4°

17 5/8"

Viewed From Above

4°

86°

19 5/8"

Front of Chair

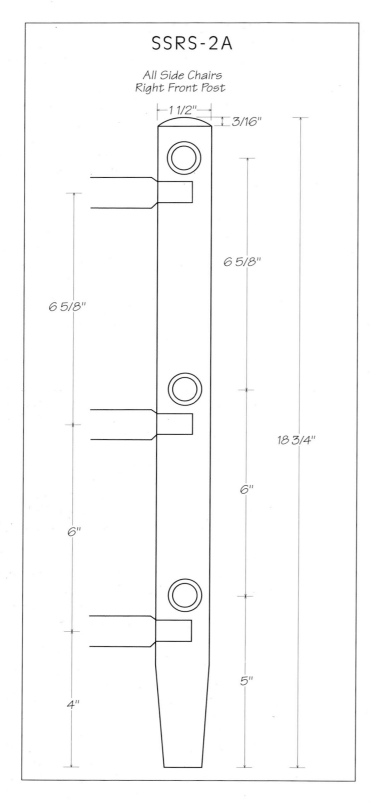

SSRS-2A

*All Side Chairs
Right Front Post*

1 1/2"
3/16"
6 5/8"
6 5/8"
18 3/4"
6"
6"
5"
4"

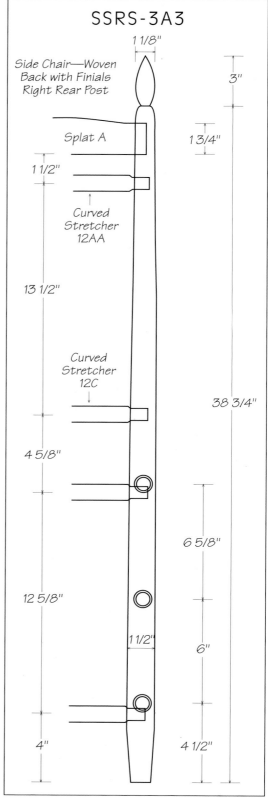

SSRS-3A3

*Side Chair—Woven
Back with Finials
Right Rear Post*

1 1/8"
3"
1 3/4"
Splat A
1 1/2"
*Curved
Stretcher
12AA*
13 1/2"
*Curved
Stretcher
12C*
38 3/4"
4 5/8"
6 5/8"
12 5/8"
1 1/2"
6"
4"
4 1/2"

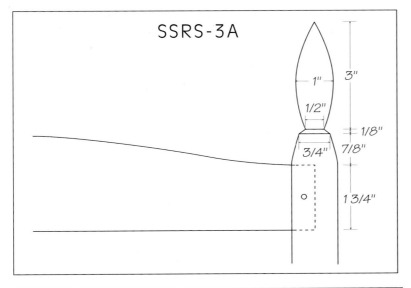

SSRS-3A

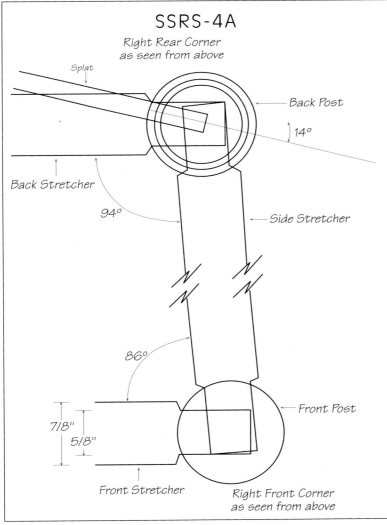

SSRS-4A

Right Rear Corner
as seen from above

Splat

Back Post

14°

Back Stretcher

94°

Side Stretcher

86°

Front Post

7/8"

5/8"

Front Stretcher

Right Front Corner
as seen from above

SPLAT MORTISES C

Make the splat mortises about 14° from the back plane of the chair. Put a router box on the lathe—see the guidelines for the Mortising Box on page 11. Rout out the mortises. The mortises bottom out at the center of the post. Part off the post waste stock after all stretcher holes are drilled and splat mortises are routed. Use a rubber backed disc sander to sand the front post tops.

STRETCHERS B

Using the SSRS-4A pattern at left, turn the straight stretchers to ⅞" diameter. Then turn the 1" long tenons, ⅝" in diameter. Finish-sand the stretchers, but not the seat stretchers. Crimp the tenons around their diameter with channel lock pliers, so they will expand in the joint, with glue, and not loosen over time.

SPLAT B

Make the splat according to the instructions for Side Chair—Ladder Back with Finials on page 28, using the same drawings in SSRS-6A–C patterns on page 29.

CURVED STRETCHERS

Follow these directions for both curved stretchers. Make a form for each, following the different drawings in patterns SSRS-12AA and SSRS-12C on page 52 for each.

Band-saw ⅛" x 2" x 21½" plies from the curved stretcher stock. Then abrasive-plane the plies down to the 1/16" x 1⅛" x 21½" stretcher ply thickness. This makes the 14 plies glue up to ⅞" thick stretchers.

To make each stretcher form, draw the stretcher's curve on the plywood pieces, as in the form drawing SSRS-6 on page 30. Remember that each stretcher has a different curve, requiring one form for each. Make certain to draw the full ⅞" stretcher thickness on the form before band-sawing it to shape. The two form faces will have slightly different cut lines, to allow for the thickness of the splat, and to ensure a tight fit when clamping the splat glue-up. Cut out the plywood pieces according to the cut lines, and then rout them. Stack-glue and screw them, following the Form Making guidelines on page 11. Refer also to drawing SSRS-5 on page 29.

To glue up a stretcher, spread glue on all mating surfaces of the 14 plies, and then stack them. Put them in between the mating form surfaces, close the form together, and clamp the form shut tightly until the glue cures.

Unclamp and remove the stretcher. After both the stretchers are glued up, scrape the dried glue off the edges, and then join one edge. Plane the opposite edge to achieve ⅞" thickness. Cut the stretchers to finish length. Make the ⅝" diameter tenon, centered on each end (each stretcher has its own tenon length), with a multi-tipped plug cutter on the drill press, with its table in vertical position. Then rout each corner off the stretchers, making them circular in section.

FRONT ASSEMBLY A
Parts are now all machined and finished, but not yet drilled for the side stretcher holes. Assemble the front section with glue: two front posts and the three stretchers that span between them. One clamp on each spanning member should be sufficient. Make certain the assembly stays in its flat, sym-metrical plane by twisting out any unevenness before leaving it to set up.

BACK ASSEMBLY B
Assemble the back section: the two tall posts, with the two straight stretchers, the two curved stretchers and one splat that spans them. Again, make certain the assembly stays in its flat, symmetrical plane

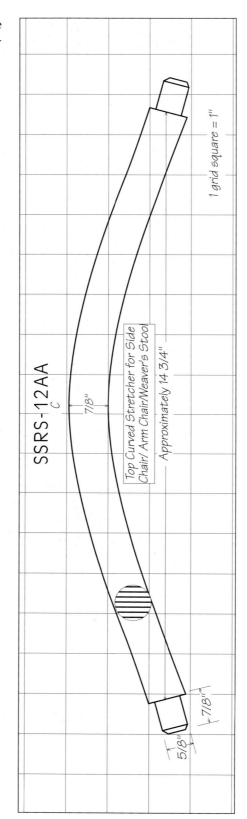

SSRS-12AA
c
7/8"
Top Curved Stretcher for Side Chair/ Arm Chair/Weaver's Stool
Approximately 14 3/4"
1 grid square = 1"
5/8"
7/8"

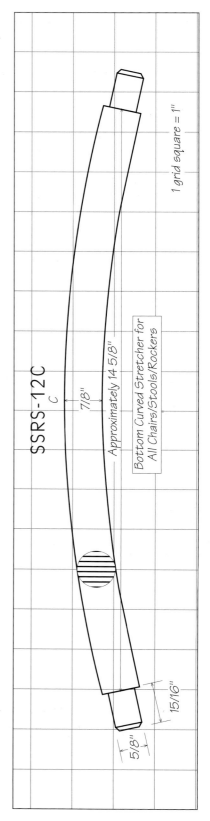

SSRS-12C
c
7/8"
Bottom Curved Stretcher for All Chairs/Stools/Rockers
Approximately 14 5/8"
1 grid square = 1"
5/8"
15/16"

by twisting out any unevenness before leaving it to set up. When dry, pin the top slat tenons with the ³⁄₃₂" brass rod from the back by drilling a hole and epoxying in a piece of rod. Cut the rod and file it flush.

FULL ASSEMBLY A

With the glue of both assemblies cured, drill side stretcher holes on the drill press about 4° off of square as seen from above, so the seat tapers larger to its front. Stretchers are all perpendicular to the upright posts, as seen from the chair sides, front and rear. A ½" tilt for comfort is accomplished now through the ½" discrepancy between the front and back post stretcher hole heights off the floor. The holes now being drilled for the side stretchers are drilled into the rear stretcher tenons. This is traditional for chairs. Then, in one assembly, glue in all six side stretchers into the front section, just before gluing them into the back assembly. Again, rack the chair to correct any unevenness, after gluing and clamping, if all four legs don't touch the flat table saw surface at once.

FINISH A

After the glue cures, apply two coats of oil and then one coat of wax.

WEAVING

When finish has cured, follow instructions on page 66 for Seat Weaving—Side Chair and page 70 for Back Weaving.

In the weave. The curve in this chair's back is definite even after the splats have been woven over with the Shaker upholstery tape.

Rejection of extravagance and excess brought restrained, if elegant, architecture and utilitarian design forms.

Sisters. Left to right are the Side Chair—Woven Back with Finials (instructions on page 49) and the Side Chair—Ladder Back with Shawl Rail (instructions on page 45).

Weaver's Stool
—Woven Back with Shawl Rail

SPECIFICATIONS

BASICS
Material: walnut
Overall Dimensions: 39¹⁄₁₆" high x
  19⅝" wide x 18⅛" dia.
Finish: oil and wax

PART LIST
Walnut

Back posts	(2)	1⅝" x 1⅝" x 39"
Front posts	(2)	1⅝" x 1⅝" x 26"
Front		
stretchers	(2)	¹⁵⁄₁₆" x ¹⁵⁄₁₆" x 18⅝"
Side & rear		
stretchers	(5)	¹⁵⁄₁₆" x ¹⁵⁄₁₆" x 16⅝"
Splat stock	(1)	1¾" x 2⅞" x 18"
Shawl rail		
stock	(1)	1⅛" x 2" x 22"

Hickory

Front seat		
stretcher	(1)	¹⁵⁄₁₆" x ¹⁵⁄₁₆" x 18⅝"
Side & rear		
stretchers	(3)	¹⁵⁄₁₆" x ¹⁵⁄₁₆" x 16⅝"
Curved stretcher		
stock	(2)	1⅛" x 2" x 21½"

Plywood

Splat form		
layers	(4)	¾" x 9" x 20½"
Curved stretcher form		
layers	(4)	¾" x 9" x 20½"
(two for each curve A & C)		
Shawl rail form		
layers	(2)	¾" x 9" x 20½"

FRONT POSTS A
Using the SSRS-1C pattern at right and the SSRS-2D pattern on page 58, make two front posts, by first turning the stock from the 1⅝" square, to 1½" cylinders. Then turn them to finish shape, leaving the bottoms of the posts with no waste stock. Finish-sand the posts and turn them off to finished length. Turn a ³⁄₁₆" high dome at the tops of the posts.

BACK POSTS E
Refer to the SSRS-3A6 pattern on page 58 and the SSRS-3B on page 59. For back posts, the directions are the same, except keep waste stock attached at the top ends of the posts after turning to shape, so they can be held while mortising and drilling later. At 28" from their bottom ends, begin a straight taper to 1" diameter at the top of the posts. Turn a tenon at top of posts after mortising is done.

SANDING & DRILLING THE POSTS B
Finish-sand front and back posts. Then drill the stretcher holes for front and back stretchers, including holes for the curved stretchers, on (continued on page 59)

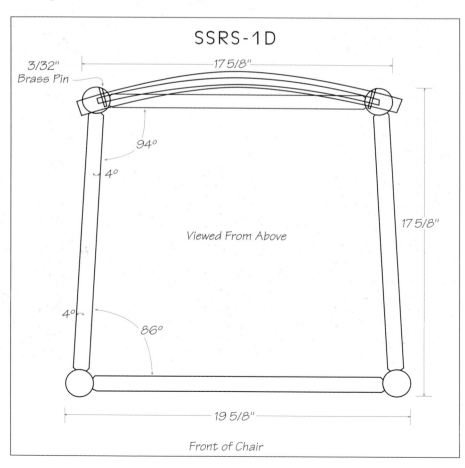

SSRS-1D

3/32"
Brass Pin

17 5/8"

94°

4°

17 5/8"

Viewed From Above

4°

86°

19 5/8"

Front of Chair

For weaving. Weaver's Stool—Woven Back
with Shawl Rail.

SSRS-2D

Weavers Stool—Woven
Back with Shawl Rail
Right Front Post

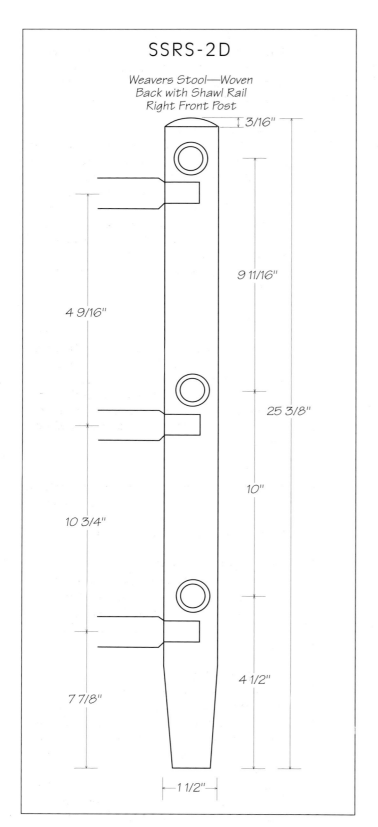

3/16"

9 11/16"

4 9/16"

25 3/8"

10"

10 3/4"

4 1/2"

7 7/8"

1 1/2"

SSRS-3A6

Weaver's Stool—Woven
Back with Shawl Rail
Right Rear Post

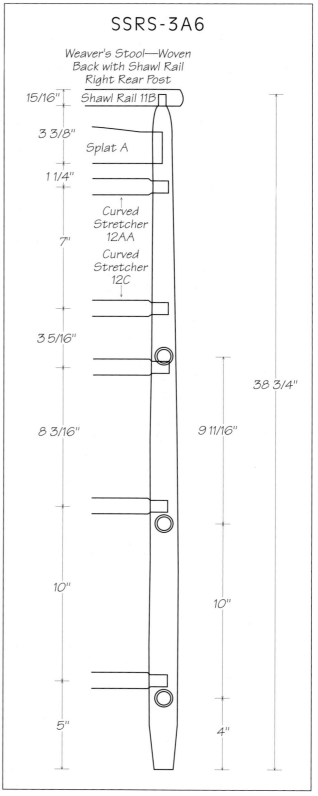

15/16" Shawl Rail 11B

3 3/8"

Splat A

1 1/4"

Curved
Stretcher
12AA

7"

Curved
Stretcher
12C

3 5/16"

38 3/4"

8 3/16"

9 11/16"

10"

10"

5"

4"

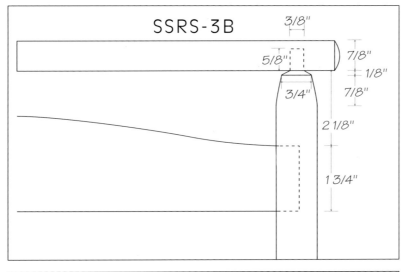

SSRS-3B

3/8"
5/8"
7/8"
1/8"
3/4"
7/8"
2 1/8"
1 3/4"

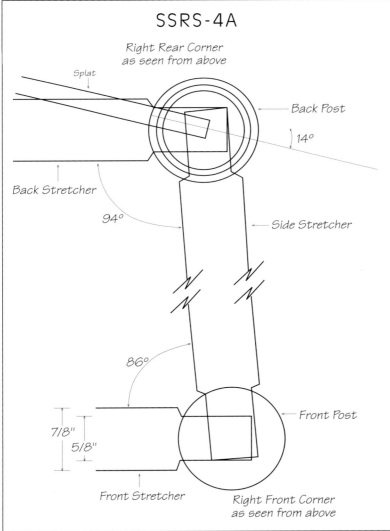

SSRS-4A

Right Rear Corner
as seen from above

Splat

Back Post

14°

Back Stretcher

94°

Side Stretcher

86°

Front Post

7/8"
5/8"

Front Stretcher

Right Front Corner
as seen from above

(continued from page 56)
the inside of each post on the drill press. The curved stretcher holes are at different angles to the back plane of the stool for each stretcher.

SPLAT MORTISES C
Make the splat mortises about 14° from the back plane of the stool. Put a router box on the lathe—see the guidelines for the Mortising Box on page 11. Rout out the mortises. The mortises bottom out at the center of the posts. Part off the post waste stock after all stretcher holes are drilled and splat mortises are routed. Use a rubber-backed disc sander to sand the front post tops.

STRETCHERS B
Using the SSRS-4A pattern at left, turn the straight stretchers to ⅞" diameter. Then turn the 1"-long tenons, ⅝" in diameter. Finish-sand the stretchers, but not the seat stretchers. Crimp the tenons around their diameter with channel lock pliers, so they will expand in the joint, with glue, and not loosen over time.

SPLAT A
Make the splat according to the instructions for Side Chair—Ladder Back with Finials on page 28, using the same drawings in SSRS-6A–C patterns on page 29.

CURVED STRETCHERS
Make the curved stretchers according to the instructions for the Side Chair—Woven Back with Finials on page 51, using drawings SSRS-12AA and SSRS-12C on page 52.

FRONT ASSEMBLY A
Parts are now all machined and finished, but not yet drilled for the side stretcher holes. Assemble the front section with glue: two front posts and the three stretchers that span between them. One clamp on each spanning member should be sufficient. Make certain the assembly stays in its flat, symmetrical plane by twisting out any unevenness before leaving it to set up.

BACK ASSEMBLY C

Assemble the back section: the two tall posts, with the three straight stretchers, the two curved stretchers and one splat that spans them. Again, make certain the assembly stays in its flat, symmetrical plane by twisting out any unevenness before leaving it to set up. When dry, pin the top slat tenons with the ³⁄₃₂" brass rod from the back by drilling a hole and epoxying in a piece of rod. Cut the rod and file it flush.

FULL ASSEMBLY A

With the glue of both assemblies cured, drill side stretcher holes on the drill press about 4° off of square as seen from above, so the seat tapers larger to its front. Stretchers are all perpendicular to the upright posts, as seen from the chair sides, front and rear. A ½" tilt for comfort is accomplished now through the ½" discrepancy between the front and back post stretcher hole heights off the floor.

The holes now being drilled for the side stretchers are drilled into the rear stretcher tenons. This is traditional for chairs. Then, in one assembly, glue in all six side stretchers into the front section, just before gluing them into the back assembly. Again, rack the chair to correct any unevenness, after gluing and clamping, if all four legs don't touch the flat table saw surface at once.

SHAWL RAIL A (SHALLOW CURVE)

Make the shawl rail according to the instructions for Side Chair— Ladder Back with Shawl Rail on page 48, using drawing SSRS-11B below.

FINISH A

After the glue cures, apply two coats of oil and then one coat of wax.

WEAVING

When finish has cured, follow instructions on page 66 for Seat Weaving—Weaver's Stool and page 70 for Back Weaving.

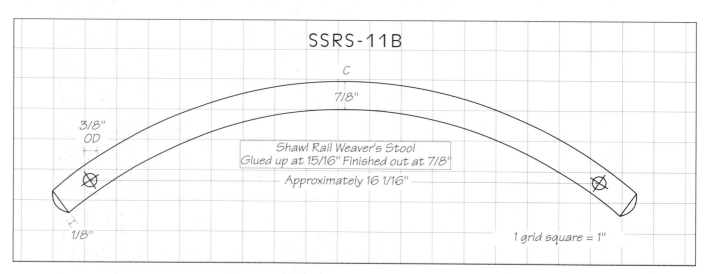

SSRS-11B

C

7/8"

3/8"
OD

Shawl Rail Weaver's Stool
Glued up at 15/16" Finished out at 7/8"

Approximately 16 1/16"

1/8"

1 grid square = 1"

The result of the Shakers' labor remains to remind us of a way of life that wrought dignity in work, tranquillity in spirit, and excellence in all things.

Comforting curves. This Rocking Chair—Woven Back with Shawl Rail is made of beautiful purpleheart.

Rocking Chair

—Woven Back with Shawl Rail

SPECIFICATIONS

BASICS

Material: purpleheart or dyed maple
Overall Dimensions: 42" high x 25¼" wide x 33" dia.
Finish: oil and wax

PART LIST

Purpleheart or dyed maple		
Back posts	(2)	1⅝" x 1⅝" x 42½"
Front posts	(2)	1⅝" x 1⅝" x 20½"
Front stretchers	(2)	15/16" x 15/16" x 22⅝"
Side stretchers	(4)	15/16" x 15/16" x 17⅝"
Rear stretcher	(1)	15/16" x 15/16" x 16⅝"
Splat stock	(4)	1¾" x 2⅞" x 18"
Arms	(2)	¾" x 4" wide x 19" long
Pommels	(2)	¾" x 2⅝" square
Rocker stock	(2)	1⅝" x 3" x 36"
Hickory		
Front seat stretcher	(1)	15/16" x 15/16" x 22⅝"
Side stretchers	(2)	15/16" x 15/16" x 17⅝"
Rear stretchers	(1)	15/16" x 15/16" x 16⅝"
Curved stretcher stock	(2)	1⅛" x 2" x 21½"
Plywood		
Splat form layers	(4)	¾" x 9" x 20½"
Curved stretcher form layers (two for each curve A & C)	(4)	¾" x 9" x 20½"
Shawl rail form layers	(2)	¾" x 9" x 20½"
Rocker form layers	(3)	¾" x 15" x 36"
Dowels		
Arm back	(2)	⅜" x 1½"
Front	(2)	½" x 11 3/16"
Rockers	(4)	½" x 2"

SSRS-1E

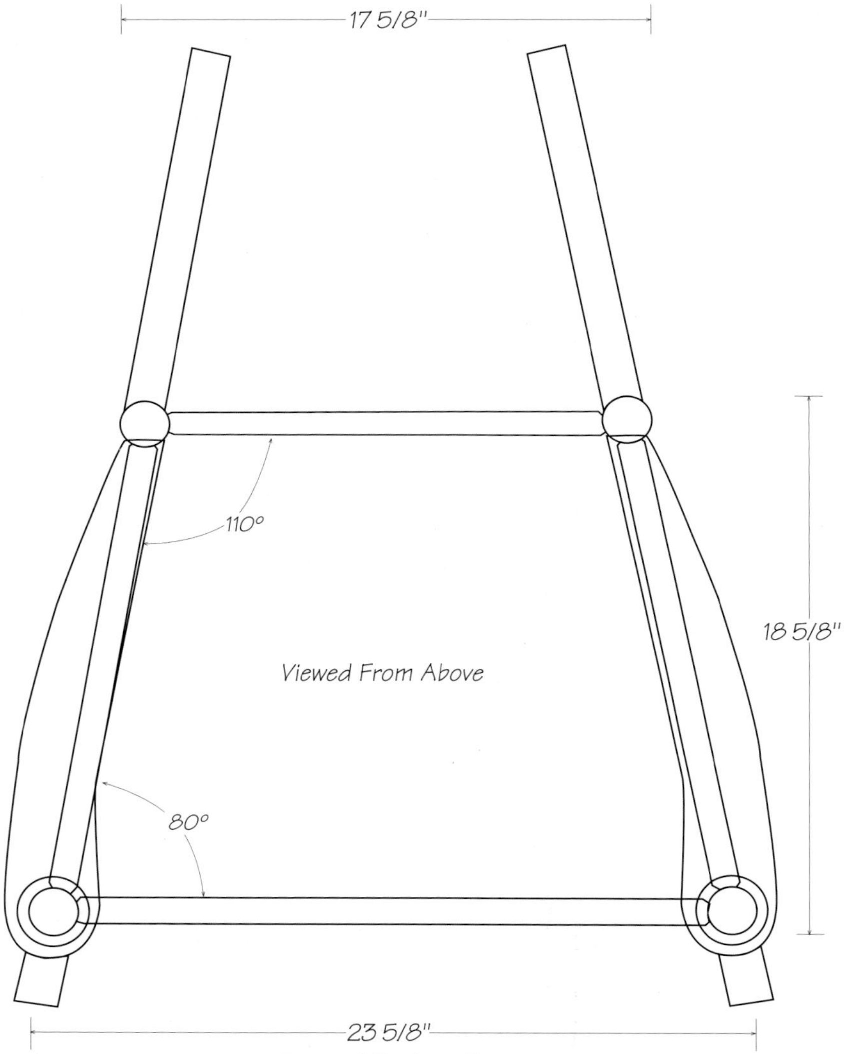

17 5/8"
110°
18 5/8"
Viewed From Above
80°
23 5/8"

Front of Rocking Chair

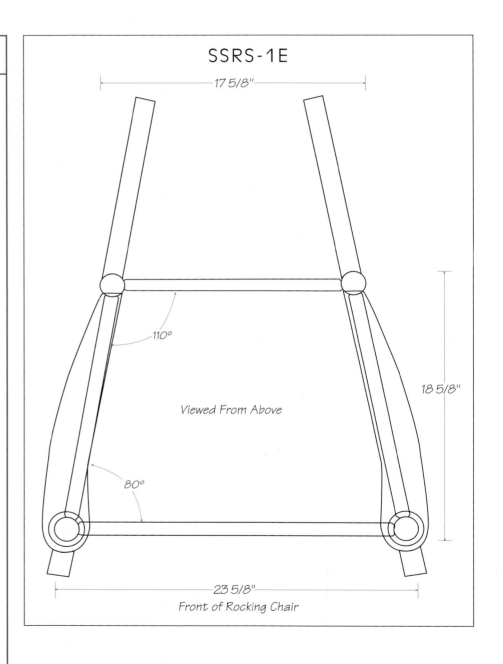

SSRS-2C

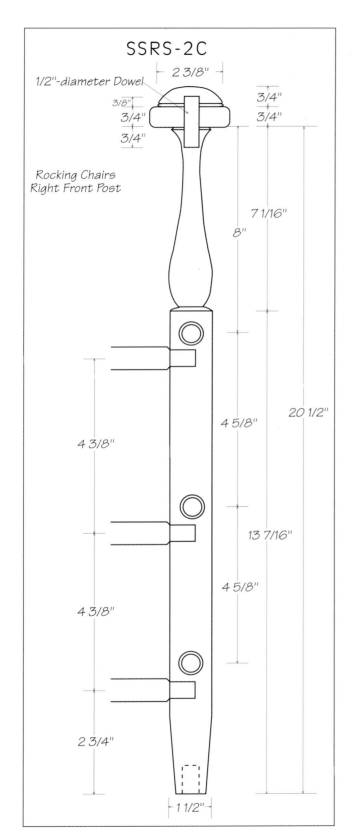

1/2"-diameter Dowel

2 3/8"

3/8"
3/4"
3/4"

3/4"
3/4"
3/4"

Rocking Chairs
Right Front Post

7 1/16"

8"

20 1/2"

4 5/8"

4 3/8"

13 7/16"

4 5/8"

4 3/8"

2 3/4"

1 1/2"

SSRS-3A7

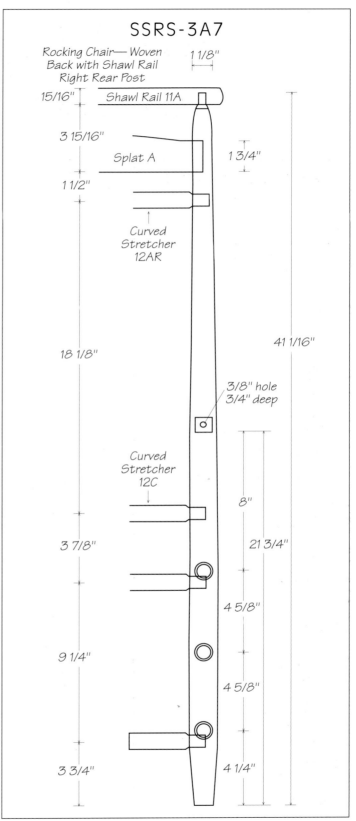

Rocking Chair— Woven
Back with Shawl Rail
Right Rear Post

1 1/8"

15/16"   Shawl Rail 11A

3 15/16"

Splat A

1 3/4"

1 1/2"

Curved
Stretcher
12AR

41 1/16"

18 1/8"

3/8" hole
3/4" deep

Curved
Stretcher
12C

8"

3 7/8"

21 3/4"

4 5/8"

9 1/4"

4 5/8"

3 3/4"

4 1/4"

FRONT POSTS C

Using the SSRS-1E pattern on page 62 and the SSRS-2C pattern on page 63, make two front posts, by first drilling a hole ½" diameter x ¾" deep in the top ends. Then drill a hole ½" diameter x 1⅜" deep in each bottom end. Lathe-turn the stock from the 1⅝" square, to 1½" cylinders. Turn posts to finish shape. Don't make any cuts now on the bottom ends—leave them long.

BACK POSTS C

Refer to the SSRS-3A7 pattern on page 63 and the SSRS-3B pattern at right. For the back posts, first drill a hole in each bottom end, ½" diameter, 2¼" long. Then lathe-turn the stock from 1⅝" square, to a 1½" cylinder. At 20" from their bottom ends, begin a straight taper down to 1" diameter at the top of the posts. Turn them to finish shape, leaving the bottoms of the posts long—wait until the end of the project to cut them to receive the rockers. Keep waste stock attached at the top ends of the posts after turning to shape, so they can be held while drilling and mortising later. Turn tenon on back posts after mortising is done.

SANDING & DRILLING THE POSTS B

Finish-sand front and back posts. Then drill the holes for front and back stretchers, including the holes for the curved stretchers, on the inside of each post on the drill press. Remember that the curved stretcher holes are at different angles to the back plane of the chair for each stretcher.

SPLAT MORTISES D

Make the splat mortises about 14° from the back plane of the chair. Put a router box on the lathe—see the guidelines for the Mortising Box on page 11. Rout out the mortises.

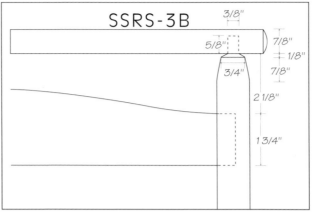

Shakers were devoted to a life of simplicity, perfection, integrity, and work.

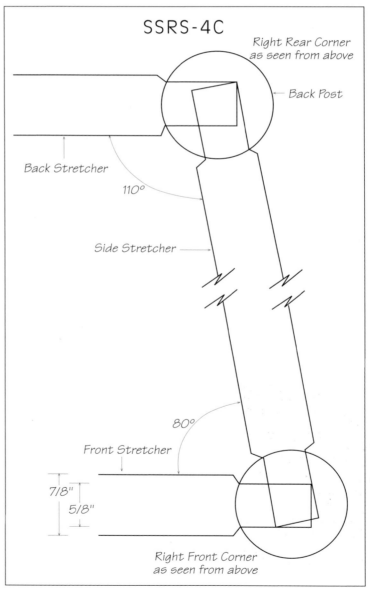

The mortises bottom out at the center of the post. Part off the post waste stock after all stretcher holes are drilled and splat mortises are routed.

STRETCHERS B
Using the SSRS-4C pattern on the opposite page, turn the straight stretchers to ⅞" diameter. Then turn the 1"-long tenons, ⅝" in diameter. Finish-sand the stretchers, but not the seat stretchers. Crimp the tenons around their diameter with channel lock pliers, so they will expand in the joint, with glue, and not loosen over time.

SPLAT A
Make the splat according to the instructions for Side Chair—Ladder Back with Finials on page 28, using the same drawings in SSRS-6A–C patterns on page 29.

CURVED STRETCHERS
Make the curved stretchers according to the instructions for the Side Chair—Woven Back with Finials on page 51, using drawings SSRS-12AR on page 44 and SSRS-12C on page 52.

FRONT ASSEMBLY A
Parts are now all machined and finished, but not yet drilled for the side stretcher holes. Assemble the

front section with glue: two front posts and the three stretchers that span between them. One clamp on each spanning member should be sufficient. Make certain the assembly stays in its flat, symmetrical plane by twisting out any unevenness before leaving it to set up.

BACK ASSEMBLY C
Assemble the back section: the two tall posts, with the three straight stretchers, the two curved stretchers and one splat that spans them. Again, make certain the assembly stays in its flat, symmetrical plane by twisting out any unevenness before leaving it to set up. When dry, pin the top slat tenons with the ³⁄₃₂" brass pin from the back by drilling a hole and epoxying in a piece of rod. Cut the rod and file it flush.

ARM SLOTS A
Refer to the SSRS-3A7 pattern on page 63. To make slots for the arms, clamp a ¾" x 26" x 40" wood straightedge across the back assembly, perpendicular to the post, next to the arm slot location. Then rout the slots with a top bearing straight-face bit, guiding the bearing against the straightedge.

Note: The straightedge must be clamped to the bottom of the chair frame so it runs off the 1½"-diameter straight section of the post and cantilevers out over the tapered section of the post, where slots are to be cut.

FULL ASSEMBLY A
With the glue of both assemblies cured, drill side stretcher holes on the drill press about 10° off square as seen from above, so the seat tapers larger to its front. Stretchers

are all perpendicular to the upright posts, as seen from the chair sides, front and rear. The holes now being drilled for the side stretchers are drilled into the rear stretcher tenons. This is traditional for chairs. Then, in one assembly, glue all six side stretchers into the front section, just before gluing them into the back assembly. Again, rack the chair to correct any unevenness, after gluing and clamping, if all four legs don't touch the flat table saw surface at once.

ARMS A
Make the arms according to the instructions for Arm Chair—Ladder Back with Finials on page 36, using drawing SSRS-8B on page 42.

SHAWL RAIL A (SHALLOW CURVE)
Make the shawl rail according to the instructions for Side Chair—Ladder Back with Shawl Rail on page 45, using drawing SSRS-11A on page 48.

ROCKERS A
Make the rockers according to the instructions for Rocking Chair—Ladder Back with Finials on page 43 using same patterns. Cope-cut the bottom of the posts to fit the curve of the rocker. Also, make up a drilling carriage to hold rockers in while drilling for dowel holes. Glue rockers to frame using two-part epoxy glue.

FINISH A
After the glue cures, apply two coats of oil and then one coat of wax.

WEAVING
When finish has cured, follow instructions on page 68 for Seat Weaving—Rockers and page 70 for Back Weaving.

Seat Weaving

—Side Chairs & Weaver's Stool

SPECIFICATIONS

PART LIST

1"-wide Shaker cotton upholstery tape

Front to back	(1)	50'
Strips:		
Side chairs	(2)	3'
Arm chairs	(4)	3'
Rocking chairs	(6)	3'
Side to side	(1)	58'

Miscellaneous
Upholstery tacks   1 small box of ⅜"
1"-thick Upholstery
    foam   (1) 16" x 21"

FOAM A

Cut the foam to the size of the trapezoid created by the insides of the seat stretchers. Cut the corners rounded off to a 3" radius arc.

STRIPS A

While butting the end of one tape strip against the back post, and holding it down to the top of the side seat stretcher, tack it onto the top of the side seat stretcher, ½" from the back post.

Referring to the SWRS-1A drawing on page 69, lay the rest of the strip over and in front of the front seat stretcher, then pull it down and back to meet the back post underneath the same side seat stretcher. Cut it off where it meets the back post. Tack it on the underside of the side seat stretcher, ½" from the back post. Do the same with the other strip, on the other side of the chair.

MAIN PIECES A

Referring to the SWRS-1A and SWRS-2 drawings on page 69, tack one end of the front-to-back piece onto the inside of the side seat stretcher, at the middle of the stretcher length, and running parallel to the stretcher's length.

Tack the side-to-side piece onto the inside of the back seat stretcher, at the middle of the stretcher length, and running parallel to the stretcher's length. Then wrap the front-to-back piece back and forth between the front and back seat stretchers, pulling it in the direction that doesn't double it back over its tacked beginning end, and beginning it on the underside of the seat. Pull it around and over the front or back stretcher to the top of the seat.

Butt the side of each wrap next to the last one, working across the width of the seat. Begin the wraps right next to the strip. Take out obvious sag, but leave the tape so it is not in great tension. When the top of the seat is all filled in to the other side strip with these wraps, pull the front-to-back piece over the last stretcher, and then under to end. Tack it, hidden, onto the inside of the other side seat stretcher. Cut the excess tape off after tacking.

WEAVING A

Referring to the SWRS-3 drawing on page 69, slip the foam piece in between the top and bottom layers of the front-to-back wraps. Pulling the side-to-side piece in the direction that doesn't double it back over its tacked beginning end, pull it out from under the side seat stretcher. Then pull the leading end of the side-to-side piece alternately over the first front-to-back wrap, and under the next, then over the following wrap, and continuing in this over/under weave, moving across the seat with the leading end.

Upon weaving to the other side seat stretcher, pull the excess of the side-to-side piece all the way through the over-and-unders, and tug on it tightly to tension it. Pull the leading end of the side-to-side piece around the side stretcher to the underside of the chair, and weave it in the same over/under pattern that was made on the top all the way across the seat. Give a tightening tug again, after all excess is pulled through at the end of the row.

Pull the side-to-side piece around the side stretcher to the top side of the seat again, and continue weaving back across the top of the seat, going over where it went under before and vice versa, creating a checker-board pattern.

Continue weaving and pulling the piece in this way—top side of the seat, then the underside, then the top side again, weaving toward the front of the chair. Keep the side-to-side weaving that has been done already pushed back fairly tightly during weaving. After the last top row in the front is finished, with the seat full of as many side-to-side rows as possible, pull the side-to-side piece around to the underside and weave it over and under three times.

Fasten the end of the piece on the under-side of the front seat stretcher, by tacking it hidden underneath a front-to-back wrap which has been pushed aside.

WATER REPELLENCE A
Spray the weaving with a water repellent. Follow the directions on the can. Spray again in about a month when the weaving has settled a bit with wear.

—Arm Chair

FOAM A
Cut the foam to the size of the trapezoid created by the insides of the seat stretchers. Cut the corners rounded off to a 3" radius arc.

STRIPS B
Referring to the SWRS-1B drawing on page 69, hold one strip roughly parallel to, and on top of, the right side stretcher, so its beginning end is 3" from the right back post, and the rest of the strip lays forward over the front stretcher and down. Nail it on with two tacks, ½" in from that beginning end, tacking the strip on top of the right front stretcher. While pulling the rest of it over the front stretcher, place its edge right beside the right front post, and then pull it back under the front stretcher, straight back towards the right back post under the right side stretcher, leaving it fairly taut.

Cut it off to a length of 3" before the right back post. Nail that strip end onto the underside of the right side stretcher with two tacks there, 3½" back from the right back post (so it is tacked ½" into the strip end).

Holding the second strip parallel and next to the first strip on the right side, begin the second strip butted to the right back post (lay the rest of it forward over the front stretcher and down), and tack it ½" in from its beginning end, and from the post.

Pull it over, around, and under the front stretcher, and straight back to the right back post, always keeping it parallel and right next to the first strip, and fairly taut. Cut it off to length at the right back post, and tack it ½" in from its end, and from the post.

Repeat the above instructions for installing the other three strips on the left side. The outer strip begins and ends at 3" from the left back post and the inner strip begins and ends butted to that post.

MAIN PIECES B
Referring to the SWRS-2 drawing on page 69, tack one end of the front-to-back piece onto the inside of the side seat stretcher, at the middle of the stretcher length, and running parallel to the stretcher's length. Tack the side-to-side piece onto the inside of the back seat stretcher, at the middle of the stretcher length, and running parallel to the stretcher's length.

Wrap the front-to-back piece back and forth between the front and back seat stretchers, pulling it in the direction that doesn't double it back over its tacked beginning end, and beginning it on the underside of the

seat. Pull it around and over the front or back stretcher to the top of the seat.

Butt the side of each wrap next to the last one, working across the width of the seat. Begin the wraps right next to the innermost strip. Take out obvious sag, but leave the tape so it is not in great tension. When the top of the seat is all filled in to the other side strip with these wraps, pull the front-to-back piece over the last stretcher, and then under to end and tack it, hidden, onto the inside of the other side seat stretcher. Cut the excess tape off after tacking.

WEAVING B
Referring to the SWRS-3 drawing on page 69, slip the foam piece in between the top and bottom layers of the front-to-back wraps. Pulling the side-to-side piece in the direction that doesn't double it back over its tacked beginning end, pull it out from under the side seat stretcher.

Pull the leading end of the side-to-side piece alternately over the first front-to-back wrap, and under the next, then over the following wrap, and continuing in this over/under weave, moving across the seat with the leading end. When weaving reaches the other side seat stretcher, pull the excess of the side-to-side piece all the way through the over-and-unders, and tug on it tightly to tension it.

Pull the leading end of the side-to-side piece around the side stretcher to the underside of the chair, and weave it in the same over/under pattern that was made on the top all the way across the seat. Give a tightening tug after excess is pulled through at the end of the row.

Pull the side-to-side piece around the side stretcher to the top side of the seat again, and continue weaving back across the top of the seat, going over where weaving went under before, and vice versa, creating a checker-board pattern.

Continue weaving and pulling the piece in this way—top side of the seat, then the underside, then the top side again, weaving toward the front of the chair. This will cover the ends of all the strips with the normal course of this weaving.

Weave the strips that start at the back posts right into the checker-board pattern right away after the first row. Continue weaving over the set of strips that start inches away from the back posts for the next three rows after one of them starts, and then begin to weave under that set of strips, including them in the checker-board pattern.

Keep the completed side-to-side weaving pushed back fairly tightly during weaving. After finishing the last top row in the front, with the seat as full of side-to-side rows as possible, pull the side-to-side piece around to the underside, weave it over and under three times. Then tack the end of it on the underside of the front seat stretcher, by tacking it hidden underneath a front-to-back wrap which has been pushed aside.

WATER REPELLENCE A
Spray the weaving with a water repellent. Follow the directions on the can. Spray again in about a month when the weaving has settled a bit with wear.

—Rocking Chair

FOAM A
Cut the foam to the size of the trapezoid created by the insides of the seat stretchers. Cut the corners rounded off to a 3" radius arc.

STRIPS C
Referring to the SWRS-1C drawing on page 69, hold one strip roughly parallel to, and on top of the right side stretcher, so its beginning end is 6" away from the right back post, and the rest of the strip lays forward over the front stretcher and down. Nail it on with two tacks, ½" in from that beginning end, tacking the strip on top of the right front stretcher.

Then, pulling the rest of the strip over the front stretcher, place its edge right beside the right front post, and then pull it back under the front stretcher, straight back toward the right back post under the right side stretcher, fairly taut.

Cut it off to a length of 6" before the right back post, and then nail that strip end onto the underside of the right side stretcher with two tacks, 6½" from the right back post (so it is tacked ½" into the strip end).

Holding the second strip parallel and next to the first strip on the right side, begin the second strip 3" in front of the right back post (lay the rest of it forward over the front stretcher and down), and tack it ½" in from its beginning end (and 3½" from the post).

Pull it over, around, and under the front stretcher, and straight back to

the right back post, always keeping it parallel and right next to the first strip, and fairly taut. Cut it off to a length of 3" before the right back post, and tack it ½" in from its end.

Butt the beginning end of the third strip at the right back post, laying the rest of it forward over the right front stretcher and down, and then tack it on ½" from its end and from the post. Keeping it right next to the second strip, pull it over, around and under the front stretcher, and then straight back to the right back post, keeping it fairly taut. Cut it off to a length where it meets that post. Tack it there, ½" from its end and from the post.

MAIN PIECES B
Referring to the SWRS-2 drawing on page 69, tack one end of the front-to-back piece onto the inside of the side seat stretcher, at the middle of the stretcher length, and running parallel to the stretcher's length. Tack the side-to-side piece onto the inside of the back seat stretcher, at the middle of the stretcher length, and running parallel to the stretcher's length.

Then wrap the front-to-back piece back and forth between the front and back seat stretchers, pulling it in the direction that doesn't double it back over its tacked beginning end, and beginning it on the underside of the seat, then pulling it around and over the front or back stretcher to the top of the seat.

Butt the side of each wrap next to the last one, working across the width of the seat. Begin the wraps right next to the innermost strip. Take out obvious sag, but leave the tape so it is not in great tension. When the top of the seat is all filled in to the other side strip with these wraps, pull the front-to-back piece over the last stretcher, and then under to end and tack it, hidden onto the inside of the other side seat stretcher. Cut the excess tape off after tacking.

WEAVING B
Referring to the SWRS-3 drawing below, slip the foam piece in between the top and bottom layers of the front-to-back wraps. Pulling the side-to-side piece in the direction that doesn't double it back over its tacked beginning end, pull it out from under the side seat stretcher.

Pull the leading end of the side-to-side piece alternately over the first front-to-back wrap, and under the next, then over the following wrap. Continue in this over/under weave, moving across the seat with the leading end. Upon weaving to the other side seat stretcher, pull the excess of the side-to-side piece all the way through the over-and-unders, and tug on it tightly to tension it.

Pull the leading end of the side-to-side piece around the side stretcher to the underside of the chair, and weave it in the same over/under pattern that was made on the top all the way across the seat. Give a tightening tug after excess is pulled through at the end of the row.

Pull the side-to-side piece around the side stretcher to the top side of the seat again, and continue weaving back across the top of the seat, going over where weaving went under before, and vice versa, creating a checker-board pattern.

Continue weaving and pulling the

piece in this way—top side of the seat, then the underside, then the top side again, weaving toward the front of the chair. This will cover the ends of all the strips with the normal course of this weaving.

Weave the strips that start at the back posts right into the checker-board pattern after the first row. Continue weaving over the set of strips that start inches away from the back posts for the next three rows after one of them starts, and then begin to weave under that set of strips, including them in the checker-board pattern.

Keep the completed side-to-side weaving pushed back fairly tightly during weaving. After finishing the last top row in the front, with the seat as full of side-to-side rows as possible, pull the side-to-side piece around to the underside, weave it over and under three times. Then tack the end of it on the underside of the front seat stretcher, by tacking it, hidden, underneath a front-to-back wrap which has been pushed aside.

WATER REPELLENCE A
Spray the weaving with a water repellent. Follow the directions on the can. Spray again in about a month when the weaving has settled a bit with wear.

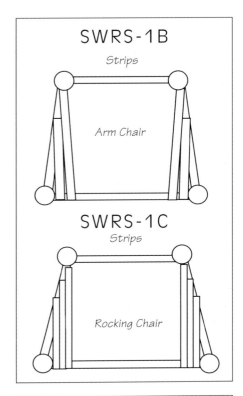

SWRS-1B
Strips
Arm Chair

SWRS-1C
Strips
Rocking Chair

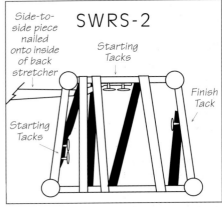

Side-to-side piece nailed onto inside of back stretcher

SWRS-2
Starting Tacks
Finish Tack
Starting Tacks

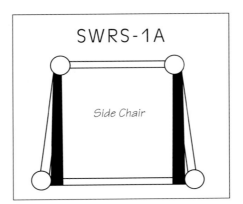

SWRS-1A
Side Chair

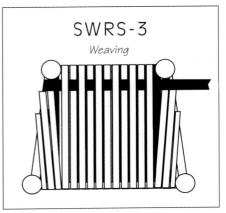

SWRS-3
Weaving

Back Weaving
—All Woven Back Seating

SPECIFICATIONS

PART LIST
1"-wide Shaker cotton upholstery tape
Up-and-down:
Side or Arm chairs	(1)	46'
Rocking chairs	(1)	60'
Arm chairs	(1)	26'

Side to side:
Side or Arm chairs	(1)	52'
Rocking chairs	(1)	60'
Arm chairs	(1)	28'

Miscellaneous
Upholstery tacks	1 small box of ⅜"	
1"-thick Upholstery foam:		
Side or Arm chair	(1)	13" x 16"
Rocking chair	(1)	16" x 18"
Weaver's stool	(1)	7" x 16"

FOAM A
Cut the foam to the size of the trapezoid created by the insides of the seat stretchers. Cut the corners rounded off to a 3" radius arc.

MAIN PIECES C
Tack one end of the up-and-down piece onto the inside of the back post, halfway in between the curved stretchers, and running parallel to the posts length.

Tack the side-to-side piece onto the inside of the bottom curved stretcher, at the middle of the stretcher length, and running roughly parallel to the stretcher's length. Pulling it in the direction that doesn't double it back over its tacked beginning end, wrap the up-and-down piece up and down between the top and bottom curved stretcher, beginning it on the back of the chair back, then pulling it around and over the curved stretcher to the front of the chair back.

Butt the side of each wrap next to the last one, working across the width of the back. Take out obvious sag, but leave the tape so it is not in great tension.

The up-and-down wraps on the backside of the back will naturally run slightly off vertical, allowing the front wraps to be vertical and parallel to the back posts.

When the front of the back is all filled in to the other back post with these wraps, pull the up-and-down piece over the last curved stretcher, and then to the backside of the back to end and tack it, hidden, onto the inside of the other back post. Cut the excess tape off after tacking.

WEAVING C
Slip the foam piece in between the front and back layers of the up-and-down wraps. Pulling the side-to-side piece in the direction that doesn't double it back over its tacked beginning end, pull it out just behind the back post, then around to the front of the back post. Then pull the leading end of the side-to-side piece alternately over the first up-and-down wrap, under the next, then over the following wrap. Continue in this over/under weave, moving across the back with the leading end.

When weaving reaches the other back post, pull the excess of the side-to-side piece all the way through the over-and-unders, and tug on it tightly to tension it.

Pull the leading end of the side-to-side piece around the back post to the backside of the back, and weave it in the same over/under pattern that was made on the front all the way across the back. Give a tightening tug again, after all excess is pulled through at the end of the row.

Pull the side-to-side piece around the back post to the front side of the back again, and continue weaving across the top of the back, going over where weaving went under before, and vice versa, creating a checker-board pattern.

The side-to-side piece in the back of the back will run slightly downhill, rather than exactly horizontally, allowing the front side-to-side to run horizontally—perpendicular to the up-and-downs.

Continue weaving and pulling the piece in this way—front side of the back, then the back side of the back, then the front side again, weaving toward the top of the chair. Keep the completed side-to-side weaving pushed down fairly tightly during the process, especially for the rocking chairs around the arms, where the tape naturally opens and closes right around the back ends of the arms upon weaving up to and past them.

No extra steps are required. Pick up the front-to-back wraps on the backside, into the checker-board pattern as they will pull out gently to join the weaving. Each side will join the weaving at a different point.

After reaching the top curved stretcher, with the checker-board as full of rows as possible, pull the side-to-side around to the back, then pull it hidden underneath the weaving, and tack the end of the side-to-side piece on the inside of that stretcher.

WATER REPELLENCE A
Spray the weaving with a water repellent. Follow the directions on the can. Spray again in about a month when the weaving has settled a bit with wear.

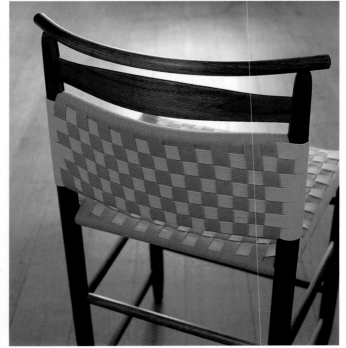

Woven details. Clockwise from top are close up views of the Weaver's Stool—Woven Back with Shawl Rail (instructions on page 55) seat, front side of back and backside of back.

Simple elegance. The ash Trestle Table viewed from the end. In the background stands the Robert Wurster's Pine Cupboard (instructions on page 122).

Trestle Table

by Robert Sonday

Refer to the TTRS-1 & 2 patterns on pages 75–76. It is recommended, on a project of this complexity, to redraw the end view and side view to full scale.

Using the TTRS-3 pattern on page 77, make the form to bent-laminate the limbs.

Resaw all the limb veneer stock on the band saw to 3/16" x 1⅝" x 31¾" veneers. Keep them in the order they came from the board, so they match when they are bent-laminated together. Abrasive-sand them to ⅛" x 1⅝" x 31¾". Each limb requires (12) ⅛" veneers.

Glue up the limbs, by spreading glue on all mating surfaces of the 12 veneers, and then stack them. Put them in between the mating form surfaces, close the form together, and clamp the form shut tightly until the glue cures. Allow at least 24 hours before removing the dried limb, to glue up the next limb.

Using the TTRS-4 pattern on page 77, make a pattern by transferring one side of the trunk's curve to one 35" long edge of the trunk pattern-cutting jig MDF. Mill the trunk stock. Trace the whole form—both sides of the trunk curved sides onto the trunk stock. Band-saw out these side curves from the trunks, leaving 1/16" outside the line. Mount De-Sta-Co-style clamps to the jig, and clamp the stock to the jig, aligning it carefully 1/16" over the curved edge in place. Then trim it to final shape with a bottom bearing flush trim bit on the shaper. Flip the stock and trim the other curved edge.

Scrape the dried glue off the faces of the end limbs. Joint and plane them to thickness. Cut the lower ends of those limbs to fit the trunk curve by the same instructions as for the trunks—make a jig to help pattern-cut this curve, and use it to make the cut to finish-fit with the trunk curves.

After milling the foot stock, taper the feet by band-sawing 1/16" over the line of the taper, and then joining one pass down to the line.

Make certain the parts are aligned as flush and flat as possible throughout this step. Make the biscuit cuts for the end limb/trunk joints. Rout the mortises and then the slip tenons for the end limb/trunk joint, and for the foot/trunk joint. Finish-sand the two curved sides of the limbs, the two long curved edges of the trunks (don't sand inside the joint area), and the top sides and ends of the feet (but not the joint face). Assemble the foot/trunk joint with glue. After the glue cures, assemble the end limb/trunk joints.

Lay the ends one at a time in a large cut-off box on the table saw. Cut the top of the trunk and the limbs to length in one pass.

Mill the crossbar stock. Then cut the angles off its ends. Rout the mortises and then the slip tenons for the crossbar/trunk joint, and the crossbar/end limb joints. Drill the mounting holes for attaching the top at a later time. Finish-sand the underside of the crossbar, but not on the joint faces. Assemble the crossbar/trunk and crossbar/limb joints in the same assembly with glue, creating the trestle ends.

Mill the trestle bar stock, leaving it over-long. Drill the holes for the top-fastening screws. Joint and plane the inner limbs to thickness. Make the upper end cut in those limbs. Rout the mortises and slip tenons for the trestle bar/inner limb joints. Finish-sand the underneath edge of the trestle bar, but not in the joints. Finish-sand the curved edges of the inner limbs. Assemble the trestle bar/inner limb joints with glue.

After the glue is cured, lay one end of the trestle bar assembly in a large cut-off box on the table saw. Place a $\frac{1}{16}$" shim under the limb since it is offset from the bar by that amount. Cut the ends of the same limb and bar off in one pass. Flip the bar and cut the other end the same.

Make the biscuit cuts, and then rout the mortises and slip tenons for the trestle ends/trestle bar assembly joints. Finish-sand the 6"-wide faces of the trestle bar, and the flat faces of the inner limbs. Finish-sand the faces of the trestle ends, but not in the joints to the trestle bar assembly. Assemble the trestle ends/trestle bar assembly joints with glue.

Mill the boards for the top, 1⅛" thick (oversize), and 35" wide x

83½" long. Glue them up together. After the glue is cured, cut the ends to 82" long in a large cut-off box. Cut the ⅜"-long x ½"-wide tongue that spans most of the width of the top's ends, on the table saw. Remember this span will be ¾" less than the stop-dado in the bread-board ends (⅜"on each end), to allow for movement with varying humidity conditions.

Mill the breadboard ends. Then rout the slots and square cornered mortises for the sliding screws in them. Rout the stop-dado for the tongue on them, then square out the corners with a chisel. Pre-drill for the hex head sheet metal screws into the top ends. Attach the breadboard ends to the top with the screws, waxing all the sliding surfaces of the screws. Mill the small ash covers for the screw mortises from scrap stock, and glue

them in. Trim them off after the glue sets.

Rip the top, with breadboard ends to width, on the table saw. Unless an abrasive planer that is wide enough to accommodate the table top is available, take the top to a local millworking shop. Abrasive-plane the top to final thickness. Finish-sand the whole top.

Apply two coats of oil to the trestle, and five coats to the top. Then apply one coat of wax to both.

Put the top upside down on the workbench. Lay the trestle upside down on it, in place. Mark the mounting screw locations on the underside of the top. Take the trestle off and pre-drill the top for the screws. Put the trestle back on the upside-down top and fasten the trestle to the top with the screws.

Clean lines. A side view of the ash Trestle Table.

TTRS-1

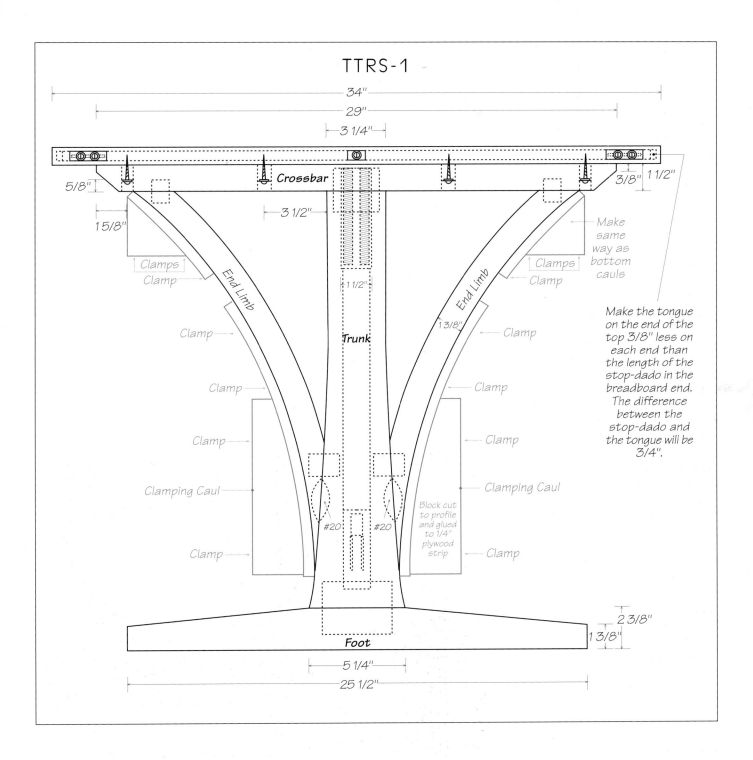

34"

29"

3 1/4"

Crossbar

5/8"

3/8" 1 1/2"

15/8"

Make same way as bottom cauls

Clamps
Clamp

End Limb

End Limb

Clamps
Clamp

Clamp

Clamp

3 1/2"

1 1/2"

13/8"

Clamp

Make the tongue on the end of the top 3/8" less on each end than the length of the stop-dado in the breadboard end. The difference between the stop-dado and the tongue will be 3/4".

Trunk

Clamp

Clamp

Clamp

Clamp

Clamping Caul

Clamping Caul

#20   #20

Block cut to profile and glued to 1/4" plywood strip

Clamp

Clamp

2 3/8"

1 3/8"

Foot

5 1/4"

25 1/2"

TTRS-2

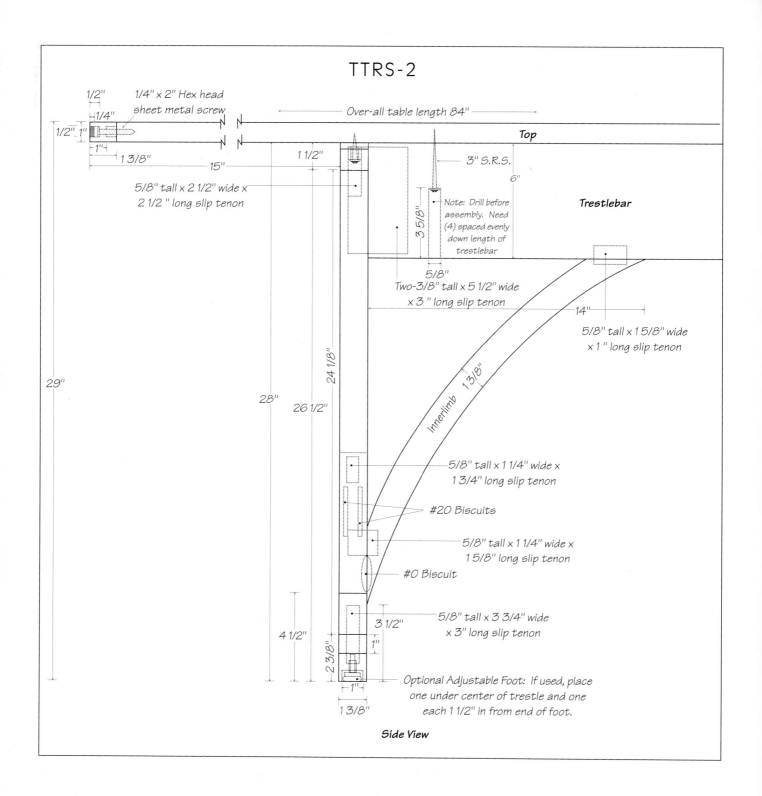

1/2"

1/4" x 2" Hex head sheet metal screw

1/4"

1/2" 1"

Over-all table length 84"

Top

1"

1 3/8"

15"

1 1/2"

3" S.R.S.

6"

5/8" tall x 2 1/2" wide x 2 1/2 " long slip tenon

3 5/8"

Note: Drill before assembly. Need (4) spaced evenly down length of trestlebar

Trestlebar

5/8"

Two-3/8" tall x 5 1/2" wide x 3 " long slip tenon

14"

5/8" tall x 1 5/8" wide x 1 " long slip tenon

Innerlimb   1 3/8"

24 1/8"

29"

28"

26 1/2"

5/8" tall x 1 1/4" wide x 1 3/4" long slip tenon

#20 Biscuits

5/8" tall x 1 1/4" wide x 1 5/8" long slip tenon

#0 Biscuit

4 1/2"

3 1/2"

1"

5/8" tall x 3 3/4" wide x 3" long slip tenon

2 3/8"

1"

Optional Adjustable Foot: If used, place one under center of trestle and one each 1 1/2" in from end of foot.

1 3/8"

Side View

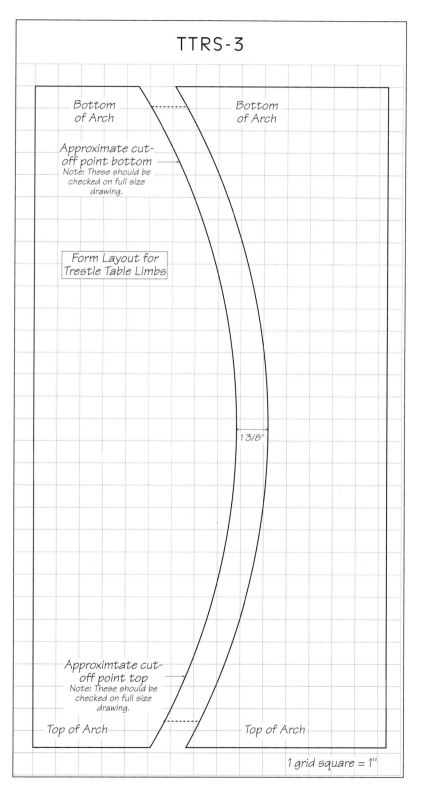

TTRS-3

Bottom
of Arch

Bottom
of Arch

Approximate cut-
off point bottom
*Note: These should be
checked on full size
drawing.*

Form Layout for
Trestle Table Limbs

1 3/8"

Approximtate cut-
off point top
*Note: These should be
checked on full size
drawing.*

Top of Arch

Top of Arch

1 grid square = 1"

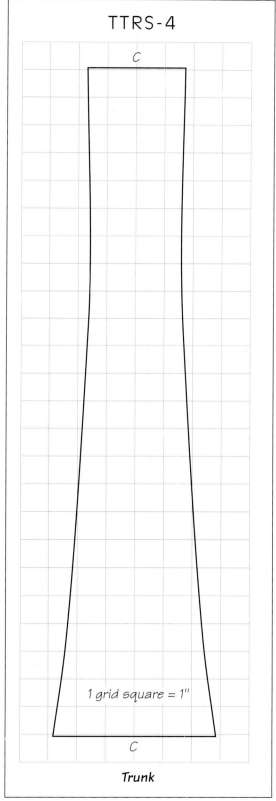

TTRS-4

C

1 grid square = 1"

C

Trunk

A meditative place. The Round Table is accompanied by two ash Side Chairs—Ladder Back with Finials (instructions on page 26).

Round Table

by Robert Sonday

SPECIFICATIONS

BASICS
Material: mahogany
Overall Dimensions: 30" high x 44" dia.
Finish: oil and wax

PART LIST
Mahogany
Apron		
veneer	(48)	1/16" x 4" x 29"
Top	(1)	3/4" x 45"-square blank
Legs	(4)	1¾" square x 29¼"
Battens	(2)	1½" x 2½" x 22½"
	(1)	1½" x 2½" x 29½"

Hardware
Metal table-top holding clips	(8)	

Plywood
Apron bending form	(6)	3/4" x 20" x 26"

Using the RTRS-1 and RTRS-2 patterns on page 80, build a two-part form following the curve of the quarter circumference aprons. Refer to Making Forms instructions on page 11.

It is recommended, on a project of this complexity, to redraw the RTRS-1 pattern to full scale.

Mill the veneers. Glue up one apron piece at a time in the form. Allow a minimum of 24 hours in the form, before removing the dried piece, and gluing up the next piece.

While the glue in the aprons is drying each day, mill the stock for the table top and glue it up.

Cut out the large disc from the glue up, for the table top. Rout its edge to the rounded profile. Finish-sand the top.

Now begin applying three to six coats of oil to the top. Since it gets more wear, it needs a lot more oil than other parts.

Referring to the RTRS-3 pattern on page 80, mill the leg stock. Cut the mortises for the aprons. Cut the tapers on the legs. Finish-sand the legs.

Straighten the apron edges on the joiner, and rip them to 3 9/16" on the table saw. Joint 1/16" off that edge, creating the finish width of 3½".

Cut the aprons to length. Remember to include the tenons.

Make a jig for the table saw or shaper. Cut the tenons on the ends of the aprons, and then finish-sand them.

Apply glue to the mortise in the legs, and to the tenons. Assemble the whole table base at once. Pull the whole circle tight together with band or strap clamps. Clean up any glue that comes out.

After the glue in the base assembly has cured, rout pockets on the inside of the frame to receive the metal table clips.

Make the three battens to screw to the underside of the table top to help hold it flat through future years of movement from exposure to varying humidity. Use slotted screw holes to allow for that movement.

Apply two coats of oil and then one coat of wax to the base and the battens.

Lay the top face-down on the bench, and set the base upside-down on it. Screw the table clips to hold them in position. Then screw the battens to the top.

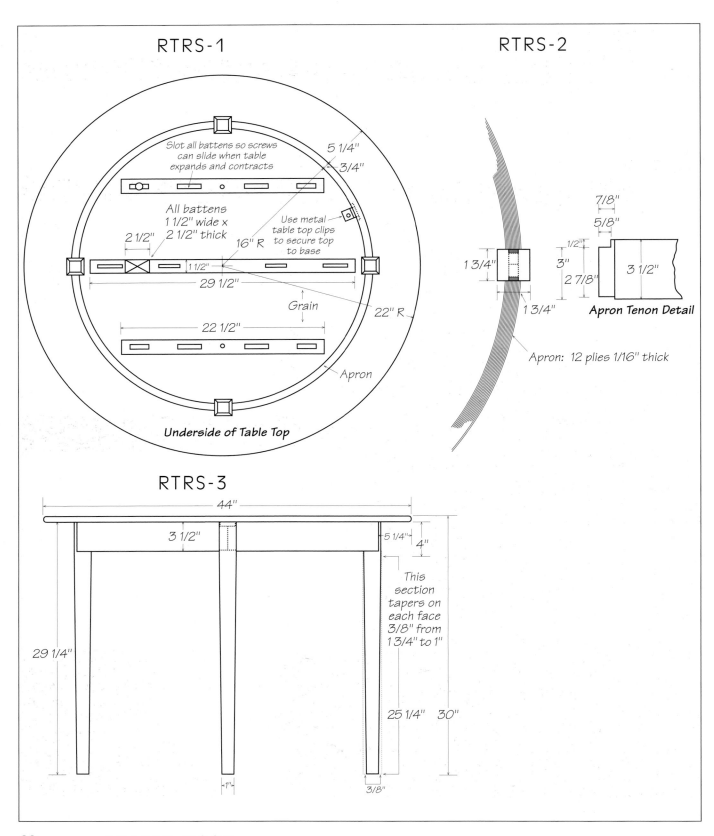

RTRS-1

Slot all battens so screws can slide when table expands and contracts

All battens 1 1/2" wide x 2 1/2" thick

2 1/2"

5 1/4"

3/4"

Use metal table top clips to secure top to base

16" R

1 1/2"

29 1/2"

Grain

22 1/2"

22" R

Apron

Underside of Table Top

RTRS-2

7/8"

5/8"

1 3/4"

1/2"

3"

2 7/8"

3 1/2"

1 3/4"

Apron Tenon Detail

Apron: 12 plies 1/16" thick

RTRS-3

44"

3 1/2"

5 1/4"

4"

29 1/4"

This section tapers on each face 3/8" from 1 3/4" to 1"

25 1/4"

30"

1"

3/8"

Storage for freshness. Cherry Vegetable Cabinet serves to hold more than vegetables.

Vegetable Cabinet

by Robert Sonday

SPECIFICATIONS

BASICS

Material: cherry, cherry plywood, copper sheet, and hardware cloth
Overall Dimensions: 41¾" high x 19½" wide x 13½" deep
Finish: oil and wax

PART LIST

Cherry		
Top	(1)	¾" x 13½" x 19½"
Face frame:		
Stiles	(2)	¾" x 1¾" x 40⅞"
Rails	(1)	¾" x 3" x 16½"
	(3)	¾" x 1½" x 16½"
Inner frame:		
Stiles	(6)	½" x 1¾" x 12"
Rails	(6)	½" x 1½" x 15¼"
Top nailer frame:		
Stiles	(2)	¾" x 2" x 12"
Rails	(2)	¾" x 2½" x 14¼"
Door:		
Stiles	(6)	¾" x 1½" x 11⅛"
Rails	(6)	¾" x 1½" x 14"
Panel stop		
15 linear feet, ¼" radius quarter round		
Hardware cloth retainer strip		
20 linear feet, ¼" x 1½"		
Cherry Plywood		
Sides	(2)	¾" x 12¼" x 40⅞"
Plywood		
Back	(1)	¼" x 17½" x 40⅞"
pattern	(2)	¼" x 8 7/16" x 12 3/16"
28-gauge Copper		
Door panels	(3)	8 7/16" x 12 3/16"
Hardware Cloth		
	(3)	½" x 12" x 16½"
Hardware		
Brass butterfly hinges	(6)	
Brass knobs	(3)	
Ball catches	(3)	

Using the VCRS-1 and VCRS-2 patterns on the opposite page, cut out the sides of the cabinet. Cut dadoes for the interior frame work, and rabbets for the back.

Make up the inner frames and top nailer frame. After these set up, assemble the cabinet by gluing the frames into the dadoes in the case sides.

Mill materials for the face frames, door frames and top. Assemble the face frame. The two stiles are made ⅛" wider than they will finish out. Glue the facing to the carcase, allowing the frame to hang over evenly on each side. After the glue has set, trim excess off with a router.

Make the door frames with mortise and tenon joints. The doors are sized to fit tightly and they will need to be trimmed to fit the opening when they are installed in the case. After the doors are glued up, rout the rabbet in their backs to receive the copper panels.

Fit the doors. Install the hinges, and then the catches. Then temporarily remove and set aside the hinges, catches, and their screws. Refer to the VCRS-3 and VCRS-4 patterns on the opposite page.

Make the copper panels. Using the VCRS-5 pattern on the opposite page, lay out the pattern on the piece of ¼" plywood. Then with the pattern on top of the layers of copper, and a scrap piece of ¼" plywood underneath them, tape the stack together.

Chuck a 3/32" bit in the drill press, and drill through the copper "sandwich" at the layout points on the pattern. Upon completion, there should be three matching panels.

After removing the pattern plywood from the top, hammer each hole in each separate layer of copper with a large common nail, driving it into the hole but not through, giving it the punched nail look. Take the work outside for ventilation and brush the panels with liver of sulfur to antique them.

Apply two coats of oil and then one coat of wax on all wood parts.

Install the panels in the doors. Install the prefinished panel stop, mitering at the corners. Reinstall the door hardware that was set aside before.

Before reinstalling the doors onto the cabinet, cut and staple ½" hardware cloth to the inner frames, and then cut and install its retainer strips.

Install the back and doors onto the carcase (including the catches and knobs). Then install the top.

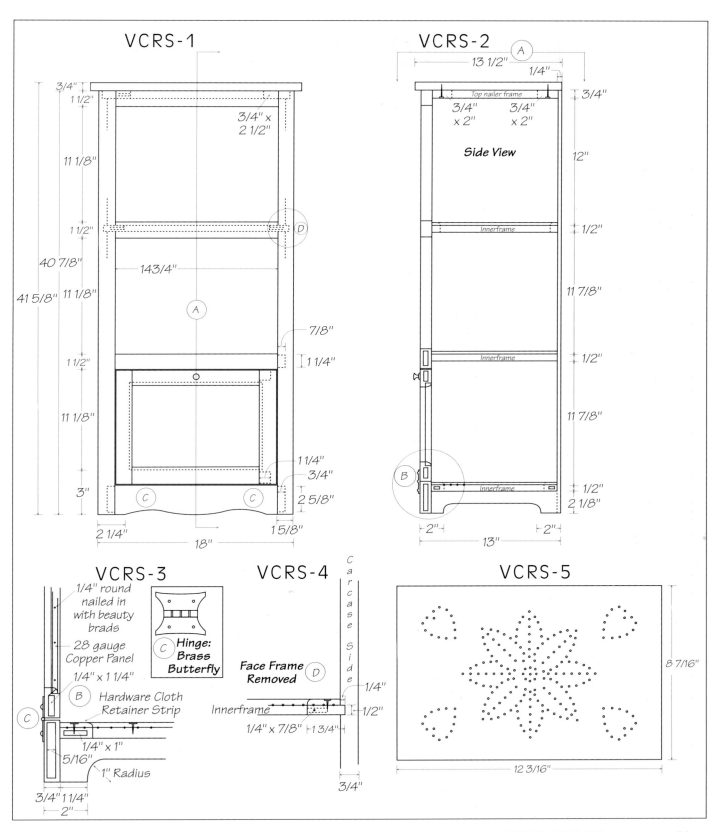

VCRS-1

3/4"
1 1/2"
3/4" x
2 1/2"
11 1/8"
1 1/2"
40 7/8"
41 5/8"
143/4"
11 1/8"
A
D
7/8"
1 1/4"
1 1/2"
11 1/8"
1 1/4"
3/4"
3"
C   C
2 5/8"
2 1/4"
15/8"
18"

VCRS-2

13 1/2"
1/4"
Top nailer frame
3/4"
3/4"
x 2"
3/4"
x 2"
Side View
12"
Innerframe
1/2"
11 7/8"
Innerframe
1/2"
B
11 7/8"
Innerframe
1/2"
2 1/8"
2"
2"
13"

VCRS-3

1/4" round
nailed in
with beauty
brads

28 gauge
Copper Panel

1/4" x 1 1/4"

B   Hardware Cloth
Retainer Strip

C

1/4" x 1"
1/4" x 1"
5/16"
1" Radius
3/4" 1 1/4"
2"

C   Hinge:
Brass
Butterfly

VCRS-4

Carcase Side

Face Frame
Removed
D

1/4"
Innerframe
1/2"
1/4" x 7/8"   1 3/4"
3/4"

VCRS-5

8 7/16"

12 3/16"

Hog Scraper Candlestick

by Robert Sonday

SPECIFICATIONS

BASICS
Material: cherry
Overall Dimensions: 7⅛" tall x 6" dia.
Finish: oil and wax

PART LIST
Cherry
Holder	(1)	2" x 2" x 6" long
Base	(1)	⅞" thick x 6¼" square
Dowel	(1)	1" dia. x 1¼" long
Cap	(1)	⅜" thick x 3" square
Slide	(1)	15/16" dia. x 1⅞" long
Knob	(1)	1¼" dia. x 1" long

Hardware
Hanger bolt	(1)	¼–20 tpi x 1½" long
Teenut	(1)	¼" long

Using the CNRS-1 pattern on the opposite page, make the holder by drilling the 1" hole longways down the center of the 2" x 2" x 6" block. Put it on mandrels and turn it down to a 1⅜" o.d. cylinder, so the wall thickness is 3/16".

Using the CNRS-4 pattern, roughly cut out the base piece into a 6¼"-diameter disc on the band saw. Turn this on the lathe to 6" o.d. and drill a 1" hole in its center. Glue the base to the holder with the 1" o.d. x 1¼"-long dowel.

While the glue cures, turn the recess to fit the cylinder in the cap blank, and glue it onto the top of the cylinder. Place the workpiece back on mandrels and finish turning it to shape and sand it.

Place a mortising box on the lathe, and cut a slot for the knob. Refer to the Mortising Box instructions on page 11.

Refer to the CNRS-2 pattern. To make the slide, turn the outside so it slides loosely up and down in the holder. Then turn the tapered hole for the candle to fit into. Set the slide in a V-block and drill the ⅜" hole that receives the ¼" teenut. Install the teenut. Countersink for the flange.

Refer to the CNRS-3 pattern. Drill the hole for the hanger bolt into the knob blank. Thread the hanger bolt into the hole in the blank. Hold it by the machine thread end in a chuck on the lathe, and turn it to its profile. Then sand two flats on the sides of the knob.

Slide the slide into the cylinder and thread on the knob.

Apply two coats of oil and then one coat of wax.

Illuminating. Cherry Hog Scraper Candlesticks provide atmosphere as well as light in a home.

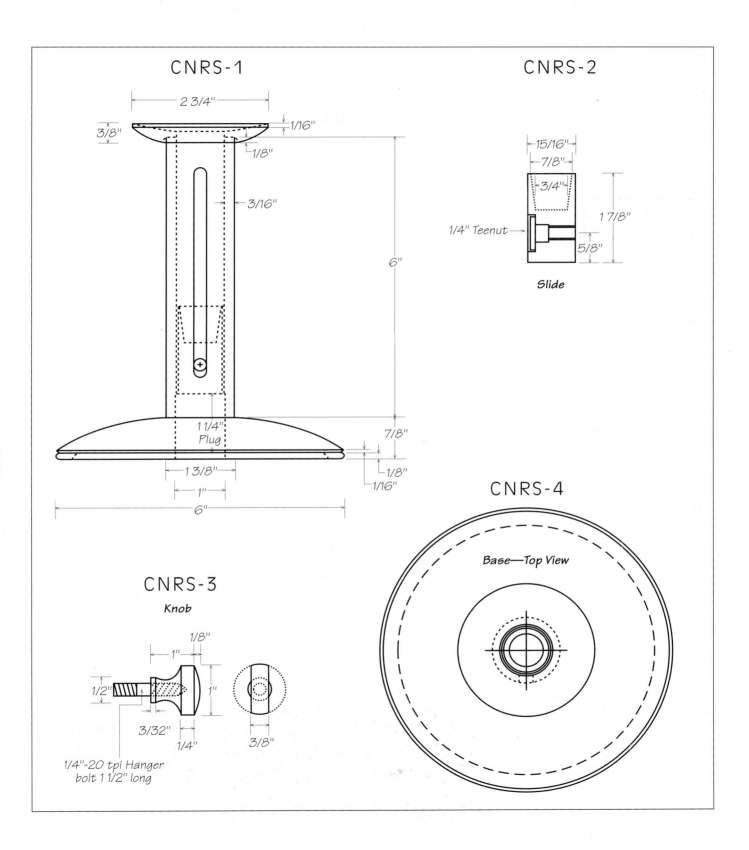

CNRS-1

CNRS-2

2 3/4"

3/8"
1/16"
1/8"
3/16"
6"

1 1/4"
Plug

1 3/8"
1"
6"
7/8"
1/8"
1/16"

15/16"
7/8"
3/4"
1/4" Teenut
1 7/8"
5/8"

Slide

CNRS-4

Base—Top View

CNRS-3

Knob

1/8"
1"
1/2"
1"
3/32"
1/4"
3/8"

1/4"-20 tpi Hanger
bolt 1 1/2" long

Pegged sconce. The pao amarillo Candle Sconce hangs from a traditional Shaker peg rail.

Candle Sconce

by Robert Sonday

Using the SCRS-1, SCRS-2, and SCRS-3 patterns on page 88, glue each face of the 8½"-square piece of birch plywood with a piece of ⅛" veneer, running opposite the direction of the outside ply of the plywood. Let the glue dry at least 24 hours. Cut the piece to an 8"-o.d. disc with smooth edges.

Cut the notch out of the back edge of the disc to fit the hanger.

Lay out and drill mounting holes in the hanger stock.

Make the rim form by cutting and then routing a 7²⁹⁄₃₂" disc from one of the 8½"-square ¾" plywood form pieces. With the other 8½"-square pieces, one ¾" thick and one ¼" thick screwed onto it, cut and then bearing-rout the square pieces to the round shape of the one underneath. Glue on the linoleum floor covering around the edge to fill it out to 8" diameter. Mount a block to the back of the form so it can be held in a bench vise.

Laminating the rim veneers together on the rim form requires two sets of hands. Apply glue to the mating surfaces of those veneers. With the linoleum sandwich strips on the outsides of the veneer stack, one person pulls the strips around, while the other places hose clamps around the assembly and tightens them. Let it set up for 24 hours.

After they set up, mill them down to finish width.

Attach the hanger to the disk with glue and one screw. After it sets up, finish the notch around the back to accept the circular rim. Cut the rim to fit, then apply glue to the disc edge, and use a band clamp to hold the rim until it is set.

Round over the edge of the rim with sandpaper. Plane and sand the back of the length of the hanger bar to match the curve of the disc.

Using the SCRS-4 pattern, install the threaded insert in the bottom of the disc. Make the slide using the SCRS-2 pattern. Shorten a hanger bolt. Drive it in the knob blank. Refer again to SCRS-4. Place bolt in a chuck on the lathe, and turn the knob to profile.

Apply two coats of oil and then one coat of wax.

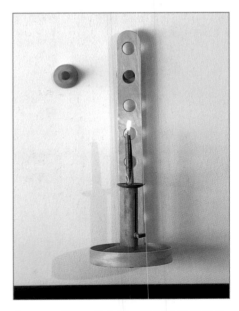

Sconce alternative. The Candle Sconce is positioned on a hanger in homes without the traditional Shaker peg rail. Refer to pattern SCRS-5.

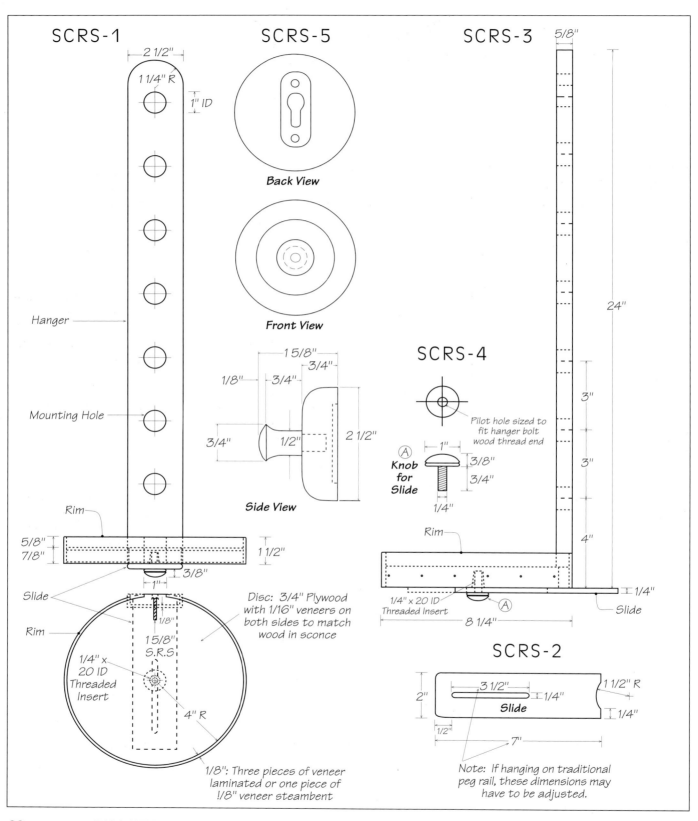

SCRS-1

2 1/2"

1 1/4" R

1" ID

Hanger

Mounting Hole

Rim

5/8"
7/8"

1 1/2"

1"

3/8"

Slide

Rim

1/8"

1/4" x
20 ID
Threaded
Insert

15/8"
S.R.S

4" R

Disc: 3/4" Plywood
with 1/16" veneers on
both sides to match
wood in sconce

1/8": Three pieces of veneer
laminated or one piece of
!/8" veneer steambent

SCRS-5

Back View

Front View

15/8"

1/8"   3/4"   3/4"

3/4"   1/2"   2 1/2"

Side View

SCRS-4

Pilot hole sized to
fit hanger bolt
wood thread end

A
Knob
for
Slide

1"

3/8"
3/4"

1/4"

SCRS-3

5/8"

24"

3"

3"

4"

Rim

1/4" x 20 ID
Threaded Insert

A

8 1/4"

1/4"

Slide

SCRS-2

2"

3 1/2"   1/4"

Slide

1 1/2" R

1/4"

1/2"

7"

Note: If hanging on traditional
peg rail, these dimensions may
have to be adjusted.

Peg Rail

by Robert Sonday

Because the Shakers didn't need to make detachable peg rails shorter than the whole length of a wall, as we do, they didn't show the ends of the peg rails. This project refines those ends using edge banding and plywood/veneer construction, to accompany the traditional side beading trim. The use of a separate strip around the edges allows for mitering corners for a clean look and getting the most out of the chosen species of wood.

Using the PRRS-1, PRRS-2, and PRRS-3 patterns below and on page 90, cut out the plywood base and face veneer oversize to 3½" x 24½", and then glue the veneer onto the plywood.

While the glue sets up, mill the banding strips to size. Always make an extra strip or two for test cuts. First rout the rabbet, then rout the round-over edges. Rout the groove that receives the veneer/plywood tongue.

After the plywood glue has cured, cut the plywood to finish size: 2⅝" x 23⅝". Cut the tongue on the board using a straight bit in the router table. Rout the face completing the end grain first and the side grain last to avoid tear-out.

After completing the face, reset the bit height, and then make the cuts on the back.

Cut the banding strip miters, fitting them carefully, and glue them on.

Make the pegs. See the instructions for Shaker Pegs on page 23.

Lay out marks for peg holes. Drill the holes. Glue the pegs in, and let cure.

Apply two coats of oil and one coat of wax.

Mount the Peg Rail on the wall by either screwing and plugging it to studs, or use the keyhole brackets as shown on the pattern.

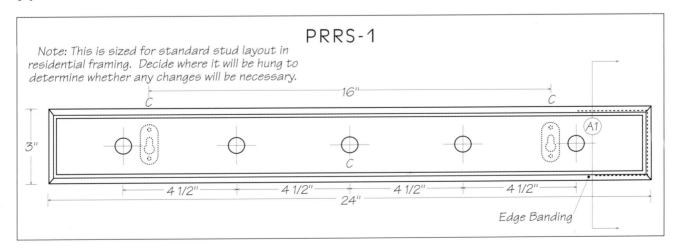

PRRS-1

Note: This is sized for standard stud layout in residential framing. Decide where it will be hung to determine whether any changes will be necessary.

16"

3"

C   C   C   A1

4 1/2"   4 1/2"   4 1/2"   4 1/2"

24"

Edge Banding

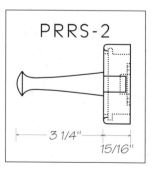

PRRS-2

3 1/4"

15/16"

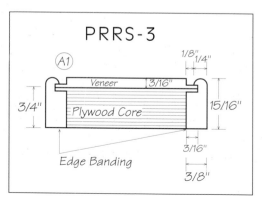

PRRS-3

(A1)

Veneer   3/16"

1/8" 1/4"

3/4"

Plywood Core

15/16"

Edge Banding

3/16"

3/8"

Shaker simulation. The small chechen Peg Rail is mounted on the wall with screws for mobility. The peg rails in Shaker dwellings were permanent — running from wall to wall.

Tailor's helper. The bubinga Pincushion offers a generous resting place for sewing implements. Its base holds hand-turned spools of colorful threads.

Pincushion

by Robert Sonday

SPECIFICATIONS

BASICS
Material: bubinga
Overall Dimensions: 29" high x 3" wide
   x 24" long
Finish: oil and wax

PART LIST
Bubinga
Top	(2)	1⅜" x 5¼" x 24⅛"
Base disc	(2)	1⅜" x 2⅜" x 25½"
Spindle	(2)	1⅜" x 1½" x 29"

Brass
| Pins | (6) | ³⁄₃₂" dia. x 1½" long |

Plywood
| Disc | (1) | ¼" x ¹⁄₁₆" dia. |

   smaller than recess of finished
   3½" dia. top disc

Stuffing
   Amount large enough to provide
   good cushion

Thin Jersey Fabric
| | (1) | 10" square |

(6" larger in dia. than plywood disc)

Finish Fabric
| | (1) | 10" square |

(6" larger in dia. than plywood disc)

Heavy Nylon Thread
| | (10) | 24" long |

(matching or contrasting color
   to finish fabric)

Sheetrock Screw
| | (1) | 1⅝" long |

Metal Washer
| | (1) | ³⁄₁₆" |

Staples
| | (20-30) | ¼" |

Covered Button
| | (1) | ½" to ⅝" with |

   bottom loop

SPINDLE AND DISCS

Using the PINRS-2 pattern on the opposite page, roughly cut the base disc to a 6¾"-diameter disc. Drill a ½" hole in its center. Mount it on a pin chuck, and finish turning it to the 6½"-diameter disc. Turn the edge profile. Sand it, and lay out the holes for the spool pins.

Using the PINRS-3 pattern on page 94, roughly cut the top disc to a 3¾"-diameter disc. Drill a ½" hole in its center. Turn it on the same chuck as for the bottom disc, and turn it to 3½" diameter. Turn it to shape and detail. Turn the top of this disc slightly concave, as in the drawing.

Using the PINRS-1 pattern on the opposite page, turn the spindle to a 1⁷⁄₁₆" cylinder, with ½"-diameter x 1"-long tenons on each end. Turn the body to its profile.

Drill the ⅛" holes for the brass spool pins. Drill the holes ½" deep. After cutting the brass pins to length, file their tops smooth. When parts are finished, epoxy them into their holes.

Assemble the top, spindle, and bottom with glue. When the glue is cured, trim the tenons off.

Apply two coats of oil, and then one coat of wax.

CUSHION

Using the PINRS-4 pattern on page 94, make the pincushion by cutting a plywood disc ¹⁄₁₆" smaller than the recess that was turned in the top disc on the spindle. Ease the edges on the plywood.

Drill a pilot hole in the center of the disc to accommodate a 1⅝" sheetrock screw.

Cut the fabric approximately 6" larger in diameter than the plywood disc.

Ball up the stuffing and place it in the center of the plywood disc. Use enough stuffing so that it hangs over the edge of the disc about 1".

Place the jersey fabric circle on the workbench with the right side down. Flip the disc and stuffing together upside down and place in the center of the fabric circle. Pull the jersey fabric up onto the bottom of the disc and staple it down all around. Make certain to take time to pull out all puckers. Repeat with finish fabric.

Refer to the PINRS-5 pattern on page 94. Using an awl, push down through the center of fabric to find the pilot hole for the screw in the center of the plywood disc. Run a 1⅝" sheetrock screw with a washer down through fabric and out through the pilot hole to form the dimple in the cushion.

Cut eight 24" long pieces of thread. Tie a loose overhand knot in the center of the thread and place over the screw head and under the washer. Pull the knot tight and bring the two ends together. Repeat for each piece of thread and position them around the pincushion creating eight "pie" sections.

Refer to PINRS-5 pattern on page 94. Beginning with one set of threads (A), bring it to the bottom of the disc and secure it with two staples as shown in PINRS-6 on page 94. After stapling, tie a knot in threads at the inner staple to keep

the thread from slipping later. Repeat with opposite set of threads (B). Continue in this manner until all threads have been pulled and stapled down. This creates the segmented look of the cushion.

Take a ninth piece of thread and tie it around the screw in the same manner as for the first eight.

Screw the cushion to the top disc of the spindle.

Cover a ½" to ⅝" button with

matching fabric following manufacturer's instructions.

Take a tenth piece of thread, lay it across the cushion and tie it down with the ninth piece of thread. Cut off the ends of the ninth thread.

Run the tenth piece of thread crossways through the button's loop. Pull on the threads and pull the button down into the recess to the screw head. Hold the button down and tie it off with two overhand knots.

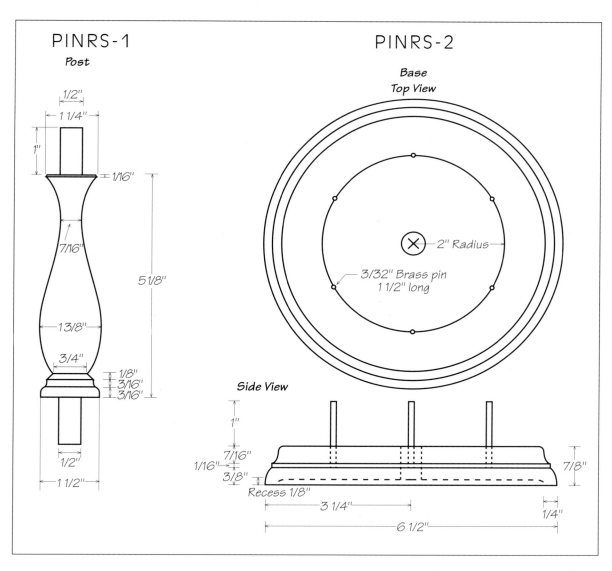

PINRS-1
Post

1/2"
1 1/4"
1"
1/16"
7/16"
5 1/8"
1 3/8"
3/4"
1/8"
3/16"
3/16"
1/2"
1 1/2"

PINRS-2

Base
Top View

2" Radius
3/32" Brass pin
1 1/2" long

Side View

1"
7/16"
1/16"
3/8"
Recess 1/8"
3 1/4"
6 1/2"
7/8"
1/4"

PINRS-3

Top Pincushion

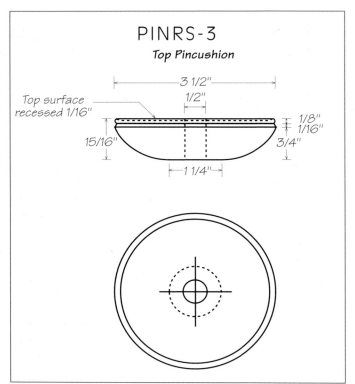

Top surface recessed 1/16"

3 1/2"
1/2"
1/8"
1/16"
15/16"
3/4"
1 1/4"

PINRS-4

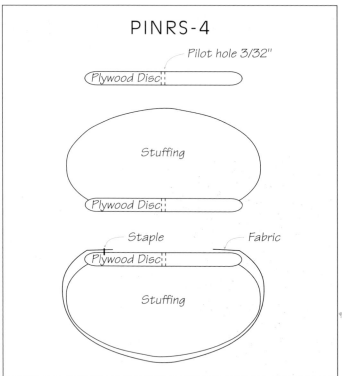

Pilot hole 3/32"

Plywood Disc

Stuffing

Plywood Disc

Staple   Fabric

Plywood Disc

Stuffing

PINRS-5

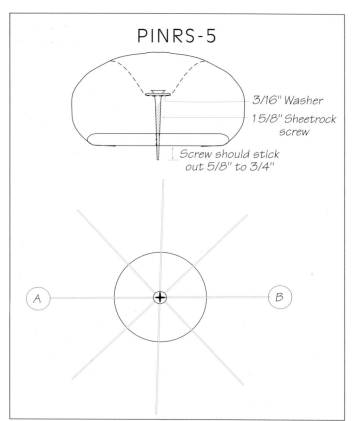

3/16" Washer

1 5/8" Sheetrock screw

Screw should stick out 5/8" to 3/4"

A   B

PINRS-6

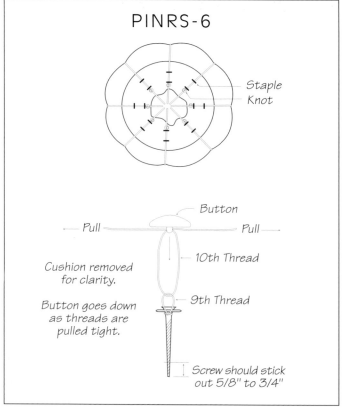

Staple

Knot

Button

Pull   Pull

10th Thread

Cushion removed for clarity.

9th Thread

Button goes down as threads are pulled tight.

Screw should stick out 5/8" to 3/4"

chapter 2

Charles Harvey:
Profile & Philosophy

CHARLES HARVEY—A PROFILE

Charles Harvey has specialized in making Shaker furniture, chairs, and oval boxes since 1984. His Shaker boxes are in almost every country in the Western world. Of all his excellent pieces, we only had room for his boxes in this book, so I will mention the other work a bit. He takes special pride in his chairs; he is the only woodworker in his shop who does the fundamental building of his chairs, ensuring consistent high quality. This high quality is an important feature for Shaker chairs, so it is nice to see it recognized as such by a woodworker like Charles. He teaches workshops in box making, chair making, and traditional joinery.

His showroom, called Simple Gifts, displays peaceful color tones and tempting items for sale. His workshop, adjoined by glass doors, is a lively yet thoughtful place to visit. He and his shop assistants can be seen working at the various stages of making chairs, boxes, and other furniture, in Berea, Kentucky.

His enjoyment of his work and business is evident in his characteristic enthusiasm. His examination of reference material and original Shaker examples shows a thoroughness and dedication to our profession that's a pleasure to encounter. ■

CHARLES HARVEY—PHILOSOPHY

In 1981 I "discovered" Shaker furniture. As I began to understand its undergirding craft ethic, things that are distinctly Shaker have driven my work.

The genius of a Shaker piece often seems to lie in what is not there. Whether a blanket chest, chair, or oval box, the work will be balanced and beautiful because of reduction of design as well as attention to detail.

I understand the balance and beauty of the best Shaker design comes from within and it cannot be applied at a later time.

Often, as my work is a direct reproduction of an original, I will endeavor to complete the thoughts of the first craftsman. The challenge of "doing Shaker" with credibility sometimes means that I must "out-Shaker" the Shakers.

Because of changes brought about by time and lifestyles, demand for design in the Shaker-style today means making furniture that honors the thoughtful approach as well as the techniques employed.

Note: At the time this philosophy was written, Charles' plans for the future remained uncertain as his workshop had been destroyed by a tornado on April 20, 1996. We wish him well.

—*Robert Sonday*

Boxed up. Oval Boxes are made of quarter-sawn maple and quarter-sawn pine and finished with several colors of milk-based paint.

SHAKER WOOD

Oval Boxes

by Charles Harvey

SPECIFICATIONS

BASICS

Material: quarter-sawn maple and quarter-sawn white pine

Overall Dimensions: 2–4" high x 5–10" long

Finish: clear finish or oil- or milk-based paint

PARTS LIST

Box #1

Quarter-sawn maple		
Box side	(1)	.060 x 1½" x 14⅞"
Lid side	(1)	.060 x ½" x 16"
Quarter-sawn white pine		
Box bottom	(1)	¼" x 3" x 5"
Box top	(1)	¼" x 3" x 5"

Box #2

Quarter-sawn maple		
Box side	(1)	.060 x 2" x 18¾"
Lid side	(1)	.060 x ⅝" x 20"
Quarter-sawn white pine		
Box bottom	(1)	¼" x 4¼" x 6¼"
Box top	(1)	¼" x 4¼" x 6¼"

Box #3

Quarter-sawn maple		
Box side	(1)	.070 x 2⁷⁄₁₆" x 23"
Lid side	(1)	.070 x ¾" x 24"
Quarter-sawn white pine		
Box bottom	(1)	¼" x 5" x 7½"
Box top	(1)	¼" x 5" x 7½"

Box #4

Quarter-sawn maple		
Box side	(1)	.070 x 3⅛" x 27"
Lid side	(1)	.070 x ¹³⁄₁₆" x 28"
Quarter-sawn white pine		
Box bottom	(1)	¼" x 6" x 9"
Box top	(1)	¼" x 6" x 9"

Box #5

Quarter-sawn maple		
Box side	(1)	.080 x 3¾" x 30¾"
Lid side	(1)	.080 x ¹⁵⁄₁₆" x 32"
Quarter-sawn white pine		
Box bottom	(1)	¼" x 7¼" x 10½"
Box top	(1)	¼" x 7¼" x 10½"

Copper Tacks	(1)	2 oz. package

INTRODUCTION

The Shaker oval box possibly best exemplifies the Shaker aesthetic. It is simple, honest, and straightforward. There is nothing adorning the box; its oval shape and carved swallowtails made it possible for the boxes to stand the test of time. Shakers made and sold nesting sets of oval boxes from 1798 until the death of Delmar Wilson, the last First Order Shaker brother, in 1960. The Shaker box is perhaps the most identifiable of all Shaker artifacts, and original boxes are highly collectible. They fit neatly into a world in which the craftsman can say "beauty rests on utility."

CHOOSING WOOD

Like most eighteenth century woodworkers, the Shakers used different species of wood to take advantage of the characteristic strengths each wood offered. Quarter-sawn maple bends well and is close grained. Quarter-sawn white pine is very stable, important because it is fitted inside the bands of maple. Too much swelling will burst the band. Other close-grained hardwoods can be used quite successfully. Quarter-sawn wood expands and contracts less, so it is used for the tops and bottoms.

CARVING

Use the patterns OBCH-1 through OBCH-5 on pages 98, 99, and 101 to lay out the box and top sides' swallow-tails on their ends with the straightest grain. Clamp the box side to a work board on the bench. Carve the arches from the point with a sharp utility knife. Carve symmetrically in ever-widening sweeps until the swallowtail is defined. Introduce a bevel while carving as it will wear better. End by chamfering the end of the swallowtail and drill ¹⁄₁₆" holes for the copper tacks.

Avoid introducing any small, hairline cracks while carving, especially at the top of the arch, as these will grow large when the box is bent.

At the square end of the band, taper to a feather edge. This will prevent the box from having a corner inside where the bands overlap. Lightly taper the inside surfaces of the swallowtails to ease their bending. Repeat for the top sides, beginning by clamping the wood to the work board.

BENDING

Refer to the OBCH-6 and OBCH-9 patterns on pages 100 and 101. Cut the form from a glued-up oval disc of plywood and the follower from a single disc of plywood. Use the same patterns for the forms and followers.

Referring to OBCH-7 on page 101, attach a 2" x 2" wooden leg to the form and clamp it in the bench vise. After the box is bent, use an anvil to clinch the tacks. Fixing a pipe clamp across the bench top will work fine for a few boxes. See pattern OBCH-8 on page 101. When making several boxes at a time, it is helpful to set a stainless steel plate into the side of the form where the fingers overlap (see the detail on the OBCH-7 pattern). Then bend and cinch the tacks in one operation.

Boil the bands for 20 minutes and bend them around the form. Move quickly, as the bands cool rapidly and lose their limberness. Mark the place the swallowtails overlap. Move to the anvil and clinch the copper tacks. Referring to OBCH-9 pattern on page 101, place the follower inside so the box will maintain its shape. Bend the top band around the box itself, mark the place the band overlaps and set those tacks. Set aside to dry overnight.

HEADING
Heading the boxes can be the most vexing and demanding part of box-making, so proceed slowly and be patient.

To make the box bottom, place the box on a piece of ¼" pine and scribe the outside perimeter of the box side. Cut to the scribed line and sand to fit. Sand one half the circumference at a time and keep the shape oval. Sand lightly and test often. Repeat to make and fit the top of the top.

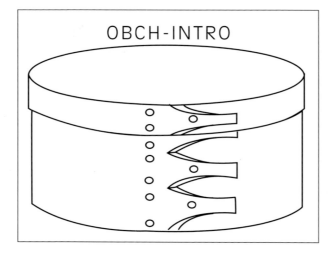

OBCH-INTRO

Boxes like these were made in several Shaker communities. They were fashioned in a wide range of sizes for household and workshop use and could hold anything except liquids.

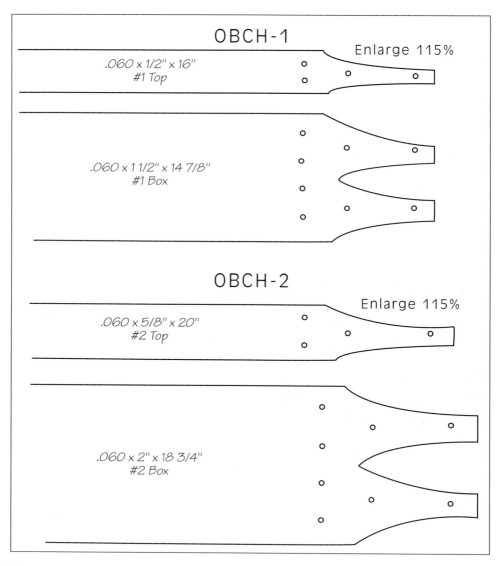

OBCH-1

Enlarge 115%

.060 x 1/2" x 16"
#1 Top

.060 x 1 1/2" x 14 7/8"
#1 Box

OBCH-2

Enlarge 115%

.060 x 5/8" x 20"
#2 Top

.060 x 2" x 18 3/4"
#2 Box

Press the top onto the box side from above and the bottom into the box side from below. Sand the top and bottom level.

Tilt the drill press table vertically to allow the drilling of 1/16" holes, 1/8" from the table surface. Drill six to eight holes (depending on the size of the box) evenly around the top and bottom. Do not drill holes in the tightest part of the bend as a crack could develop there. Insert half of a tapered round toothpick in each hole. Clip them with linesman pliers and cut them flush with a chisel.

SANDING & FINISHING
Clear finishes and both oil- and milk-based paints are historically correct to use. The important factor to remember is that the boxes must be well sanded in preparation for finishing. Take care to keep the swallowtails crisp. Do not round them over too much.

The distinctive finger-shaped joint on the side was borrowed from the outside world and perfected so that the space between the fingers allowed the thin side to expand and contract naturally through the seasons with less risk of buckling than a straight seam.

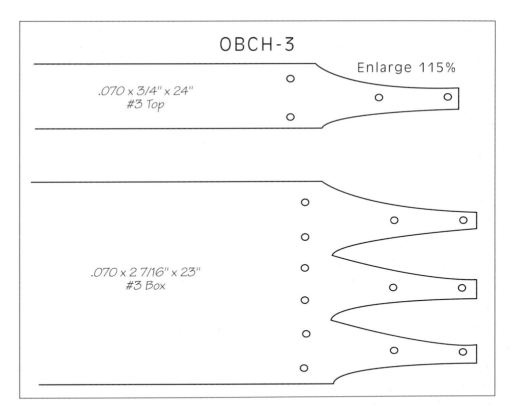

OBCH-3

Enlarge 115%

.070 x 3/4" x 24"
#3 Top

.070 x 2 7/16" x 23"
#3 Box

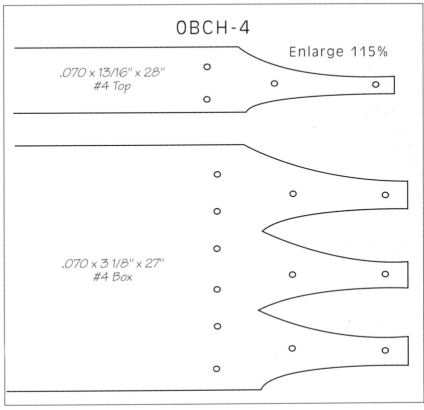

OBCH-4

Enlarge 115%

.070 x 13/16" x 28"
#4 Top

.070 x 3 1/8" x 27"
#4 Box

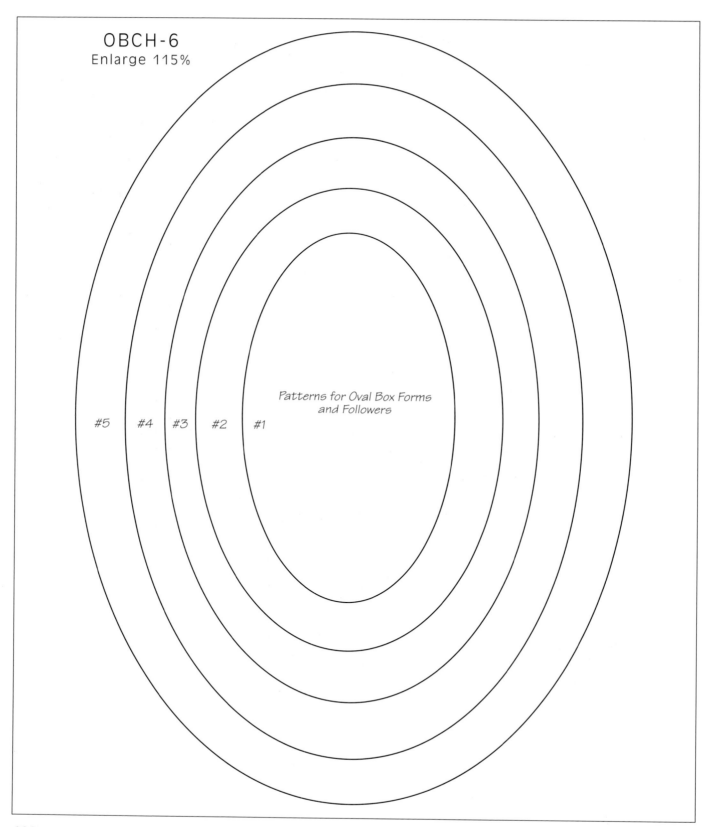

OBCH-6
Enlarge 115%

Patterns for Oval Box Forms
and Followers

#5 #4 #3 #2 #1

OBCH-5

Enlarge 115%

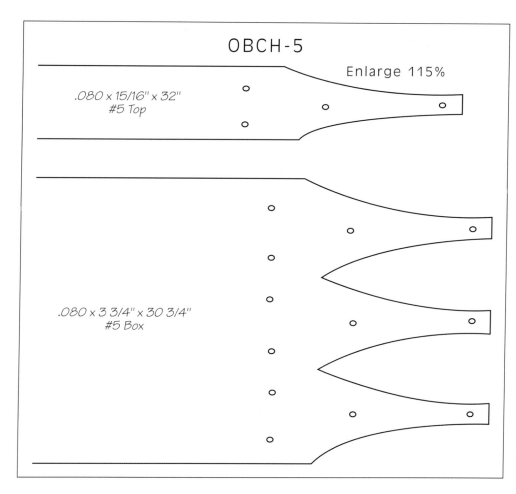

.080 x 15/16" x 32"
#5 Top

.080 x 3 3/4" x 30 3/4"
#5 Box

OBCH-7

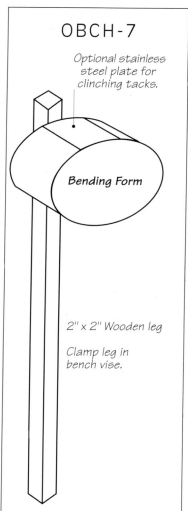

Optional stainless
steel plate for
clinching tacks.

Bending Form

2" x 2" Wooden leg

Clamp leg in
bench vise.

OBCH-8

Anvil
Pipe welded to 1/4" plate.
This clamps in bench vise for
use with forms without anvils
built in.

Pipe

1/4" plate

OBCH-9

Followers
Make several for each size box.
These go into boxes as soon as they
are bent. The holes help with putting
them in and taking them out. They
also help the drying process.
Use exact dimensions provided in
pattern OBCH-6. Then drill two holes.

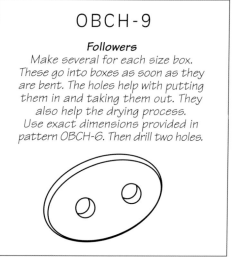

chapter 3

Kelly Mehler:
Profile & Philosophy

KELLY MEHLER—A PROFILE

Kelly Mehler is well known for his excellence in woodworking and his extensive writing on the subject, which includes his own book, *The Table Saw Book*, plus his two videos on woodworking. He also teaches and consults throughout the United States on woodworking and using safety. It is a pleasure to show his handsome work here. Often his pieces evolve from a single flitch, which enables a special match and flow of grain. His shop is filled with wonderful old machinery, choice new machinery, inspiring stacks of flitches, and a supportive array of hand and power tools.

Kelly trained for his career at Berea College and the Ohio College of Applied Science. In 1978 he opened his custom furniture-making studio in Berea, Kentucky.

Being a part of the nationally known Berea crafts scene is second nature to Kelly, who emanates the unique welcoming, supportive, and constructive spirit of so many good crafts communities—be they national, cyberspacial, or local. The world needs more of this spirit. ■

—Robert Sonday

KELLY MEHLER—PHILOSOPHY

My main interest and focus in furniture making is to make each piece to the best of my accumulated abilities while meeting the needs of the client.

I want the furniture I make to bring pleasure to me while I am building it and to the customer who is purchasing it, and I want it to be made so that it will remain beautiful and functional for hundreds of years.

The structural integrity of the piece comes from choosing appropriate joinery. The beauty comes from a combination of proportion, function, and wood matching. What probably stands out the most is the strong visual unity in each piece. This is because the wood for each piece of furniture is matched from boards out of the same tree. This not only gives each piece a homogeneity of natural color and grain, but it gives me the opportunity to use repeating grain patterns in a way that enhances the design of the furniture. ■

Unpretentious. The cherry Chest of Drawers
is a handsome and versatile piece of furniture.

Chest of Drawers

by Kelly Mehler

CHOOSING WOOD

Gather material with similar figure and color. Rough-cut the parts following the dimensions given in the part list. Glue up the top and sides of the carcase first, being careful to align the butt joints so that the wide panels won't have to be replaned.

SIDES & FRAMES

Refer to CDKM-1, CDKM-2, and CDKM-3 on pages 106 and 107. The chest of drawers is held together with seven interior frames. Each drawer rides on a mortised and tenoned frame that is housed in the chest sides. The front and rear rails of the frame are joined to the sides with a slotted dovetail and the side rails are housed in dadoes.

To lay out and rout the dadoes and dovetail slots in the sides, clamp the front edges together on a flat surface. Measure and mark where each frame will go. Rout the 2" stopped dovetail slots by guiding the router base along a straightedge clamped to the sides.

For the back slots, rout to the end mark and then let the router come to a complete stop. Now back the router out to the slot.

For the front slots, plunge the ½" dovetail bit into the sides just before the slot. Rout to the stop mark on the opposite side and again let the router stop. Then back it out through the point of entry. The side rail will cover the entry point.

Before moving the straightedge to the next position, use another router with the same size base to cut the ¾" dadoes ³⁄₁₆" deep for the side rails. For the rails, cut matching dovetails on the router table using the same dovetail bit, a tall auxiliary fence, and a finger-board. Once the dovetails are cut and fit, mortise the front and back rails to receive the side and center rails. When adding dust panels, the insides of the rails will need to be grooved using a dado blade and finger board at the table saw.

From shoulder to shoulder, the side and center rails are cut ¼" shorter than the distance between the front and rear rails. This will allow for

the seasonal wood movement of the solid chest sides.

Use both the table saw and router table to cut the tenons. Cut the shoulders on the table saw, and then remove the waste from each cheek on the router table. Set the height of the cutter on both machines so that a pass on opposite faces will leave tenon in the middle that is a nice, snug fit in the mortise.

The top front and back rails join with a single broad dovetail into the top of each side. Lay them out with a bevel gauge, cut them on the band saw, and trim the dovetails with a sharp chisel. Cut a matching socket in the top of the sides using a back saw and chisel. Reinforce this dovetail with a screw at final

assembly. A center rail is added as a kicker to keep the drawer from dropping down as it is opened.

ASSEMBLY
Glue each of the front drawer rails flush with the front of the chest sides. Then turn the case over and glue the center and side rails into their corresponding mortises. Do not glue the side rails into the case sides. If using dust panels, insert them now. Glue the back rails in the dovetail slots flush with the rabbet for the back, but don't glue the rear tenons into the mortises. There should be a gap between the rear shoulders of the rails and the back rail for seasonal movement.

DRAWERS
The drawers have traditional details: dovetailed corners, French

bottom, and turned knobs with a wedged tenon as shown on pattern DKKM-1 on page 107. The bottom fits into grooves in the front and the sides and is fastened to the drawer back with a screw. The grain of the bottom panel runs across the width of the drawer and the screw holes are slotted to allow the solid wood panel to expand and contract across the grain. The larger drawer bottoms are divided for two panels and provide added strength.

Resaw the drawer sides, backs, and bottoms from thicker stock and match the grain. Rout the grooves for the bottom before laying out the dovetails as a reminder to position a tail over the groove.

After the dovetails have been cut, trimmed and properly fit, shape the top edge of the drawer parts with a router to give the drawer a more delicate appearance. Be certain that the drawer is square and sits flat when it is assembled to avoid trouble when fitting the drawer to the chest.

Fit the drawer stops, positioning them so that each drawer is flush with the drawer opening. With all the drawers wedged in place in the case, sand the drawer fronts to ensure that they are flush. Finally, trim 1/64" from the front edges of the drawer stops so that each drawer front is recessed 1/64" and slightly round the edges of the drawer and drawer opening with sand paper.

When turning the drawer knob on the lathe, include a 1/2" tenon. Saw a groove in the tenon across the grain (for a wedge) and glue and wedge the knob into the drawer front.

FRAME AND PANEL BACK
The frame and panel back is mortised and tenoned together and grooved for the four thin panels. It is screwed into the

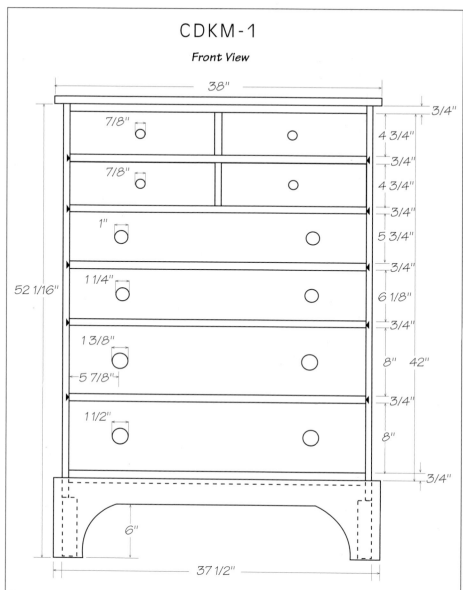

rabbet on the back of the sides but not glued.

BASE
Cut the parts for the base so that the case fits inside perfectly from side to side but has extra room at the back. Cut and fit the through dovetails and then rout the cove

molding with a 1/2" cove molding bit. Draw and cut the curves in the base. After gluing the base together, screw on the corner blocks that the chest side will rest on. Attach the base to the sides with one screw at the chest front and one in a slot in the middle of the base on each side.

CDKM-2

Frame and Panel Back

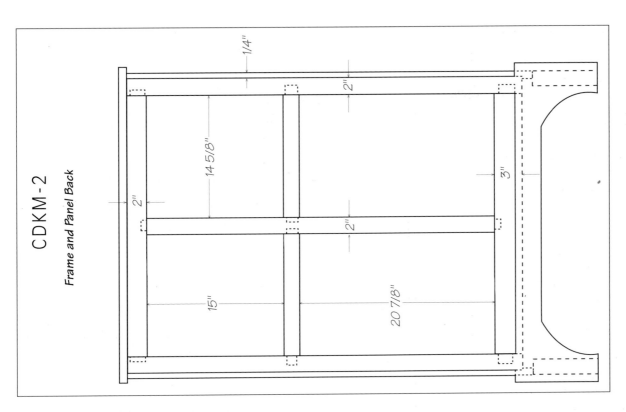

CDKM-3

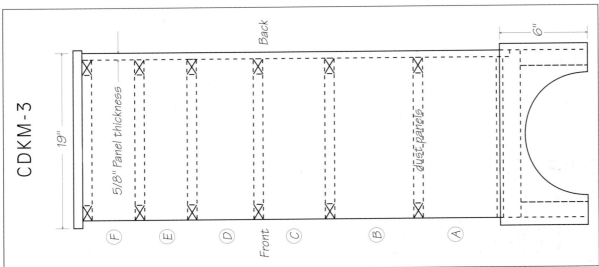

DKKM-1

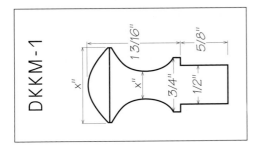

Shaker furniture makers often made pieces in multiples of two or more which not only ensured efficiency but also uniformity—a quality prized by the Shakers.

On the side. The curly ash Side Table is the perfect companion piece to any ensemble.

Side Table

by Kelly Mehler

CHOOSING WOOD

Look over the wood to be used for the table. Using chalk, roughly mark out the parts that are needed. Proceed slowly when doing so to decide where the best available grain figure should appear in the table. The visual impact of the finished table depends largely on the layout decisions. Choose the wood for the top first as it is the largest and most visible piece.

LEGS

Refer to the CAKM-1 and CAKM-2 patterns on page 111. After sawing and planing the legs to the dimensions provided in the part list, decide which two will be the front legs and which way they will face. Mark the faces of the legs that will be mortised. Remember that the rear legs get two mortises, but the front legs are mortised only for the side aprons.

Cut the mortises in the legs with a plunge router and fence. Lay out a mortise on one marked face and then transfer the top and bottom lines to the marked faces on the other legs using a square. Clamp three legs side by side in a bench vise or on the bench to provide a flat surface for the router base. The middle leg of the three is the one that will be mortised, so the first setup will have the leg with the fully laid-out mortise in the middle.

Set the router fence to ride against one of the outside legs. Adjust the router's plunge depth turret to make the full cut in about three steps. Note that the mortises are not centered in the width of the legs; half of them are off center one way and half the other way. All the mortises can be cut with the same fence setting by rearranging the legs in the vise.

Once the legs are mortised, taper them on their two inner sides on the jointer. Lower the infeed table to about a ⅛" cut. Then clamp a stop block on the infeed table so that when the bottom of a leg is butted against the stop block, about 5" of the top of the leg extends past the high point of the cutter-head over the outfeed table. The stop block is only about ⅜" thick to leave room for a push stick to grab the bottom of the leg.

Start the cut by lowering the leg onto the spinning cutter while the foot of the leg is positioned against the stop block. By making repetitive passes in this manner, a taper is created. When both tapers are completed on all four legs, move on to the aprons and rails.

APRONS AND RAILS

Use both the table saw and router table to cut the tenons on the aprons. Cut the shoulders on the table saw. Remove the waste from the cheeks on the router table. Set the height of the cutter on both machines so that a pass on opposite faces will leave a tenon in the middle that is a nice, snug fit in the mortise.

After cutting the tenons, take a piece of coarse cloth abrasive (like a piece of sanding belt) and use a shoe-shine action to round the tenons to fit the routed mortises. A wood rasp also works well. Finally, bevel the ends of the tenons that join inside the rear legs so that the tenons don't interfere with each other inside the mortises.

The drawer rails are the next pieces to fit. Both drawer rails are dovetailed into the front legs, but in different ways. The bottom rail joins with a sliding dovetail; the top rail joins with a single broad dovetail into the top of the leg.

Cut the sliding dovetail socket by clamping the two front legs together, front face to front face. Clamp a fence across the inside faces to guide a router. Use a ½" dovetail bit and make the socket ½" deep. The center line of this cut must coincide with the center line of the drawer rail.

On the router table, cut the matching dovetails on the ends of the bottom rail. Use a tall fence and a square-cornered backing/pushing board to guide the rail, on end, past the bit. Move the fence to adjust the width of the dovetail for a proper fit in the socket.

The top rail gets flat dovetails. Lay them out with a bevel gauge, cut them on the band saw, and trim the dovetails with a sharp chisel. Reinforce this dovetail with a screw at final assembly.

With rails fitted, measure the openings to make the drawer. The drawer is supported in this opening by two drawer guides screwed to the side aprons with countersunk screws. Measure the actual table before cutting the guides to the dimension given in the drawing. Adjust as necessary.

MAKING THE DRAWER
The drawer has traditional details: dovetailed corners, French bottom, and a turned knob with a wedged tenon. The bottom fits into grooves in the front and the sides and is fastened to the drawer back with a screw. The grain of the bottom panel runs across the width of the drawer and the screw holes are slotted to allow the panel to expand

and contract across the grain.

Resaw the drawer sides, back, and bottom from thicker stock and match the grain. Rout the grooves for the bottom before laying out the dovetails as a reminder to position a tail over the groove.

After the dovetails have been cut, trimmed, and properly fit, shape the top edge of the drawer parts with a router to give the drawer a more delicate appearance. Make certain that the drawer is square and sits flat when assembling it to avoid problems when fitting the drawer to the table.

Fit the drawer stops as shown in pattern CAKM-3 below, positioning them so that the drawer is flush with the drawer opening. With the drawer in place, sand the drawer front and table front at the same time to ensure that they are flush. Finally, trim ¹⁄₆₄" from the front edges of the drawer stops so the drawer front is recessed ¹⁄₆₄".

The gap between the drawer front and the table should be even all around the opening. To adjust the gap at the bottom to match the

sides and top, plane only the bottom edge of the drawer front. The plane doesn't touch the bottom of the drawer sides. Slightly round the edges of the drawer and drawer opening with sandpaper.

When turning the drawer knob on the lathe, include a ³⁄₈" tenon as shown on pattern DKKM-1 on page 107. Saw a groove in the tenon (for a wedge). Glue and wedge the knob into the drawer front. To keep this short drawer from coming all the way out of the table, loosely screw a small turn-cleat to the inside edge of the top rail to act as a drawer retainer. The cleat must be swung up to remove the drawer.

PEG JOINTS
When the table is fully assembled and the glue is dry, pin the mortise and tenon joints with square pegs. Drill two ³⁄₁₆" holes through each joint. Use a ³⁄₁₆" drill to set the distance between the fence and the blade on the table saw, and rip out lengths of ³⁄₁₆"-square peg stock. Square up the tops of the holes with a small chisel and glue in the pegs. Then saw off the excess and pare them flush with a chisel.

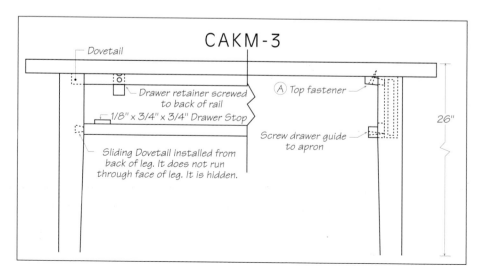

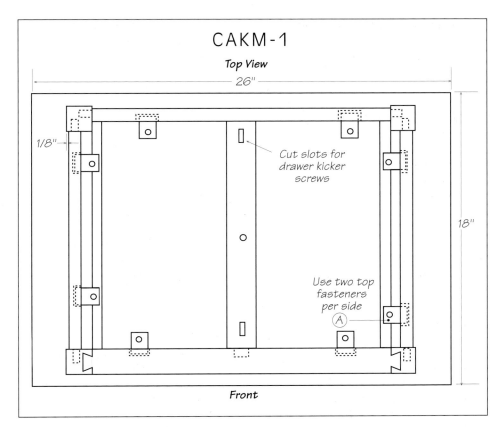

CAKM-1

Top View

26"

18"

1/8"

Cut slots for
drawer kicker
screws

Use two top
fasteners
per side

(A)

Front

Shaker Brethren usually made furniture in the winter months when work on the farm was slowed. Furniture makers were not strictly of this profession. They spent their time doing a wide range of jobs during the course of the year. It is a testament to their commitment to perfection in every kind of work that these "occasional" products possess such grace.

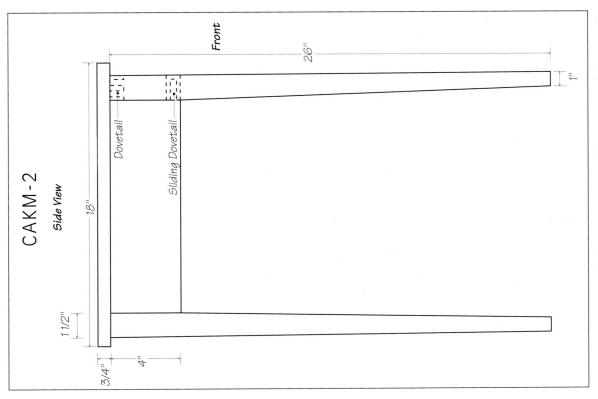

CAKM-2

Side View

Front

26"

1"

18"

Dovetail

Sliding Dovetail

1 1/2"

3/4"

4"

Shaker living. The curly maple Sofa Table is a beautiful piece standing alone.

Sofa Table

by Kelly Mehler

SPECIFICATIONS

BASICS

Material: curly maple
Overall Dimensions: 26⅝" high x 15" wide x 60" long
Finish: lacquer

PART LIST

Curly maple		
Top	(1)	¾" x 15" x 60"
Side apron	(2)	¾" x 4" x 11¾"
Back apron	(1)	¾" x 4" x 55½"
Legs	(4)	1½" x 1½" x 25⅞"
Bottom rail	(1)	¾" x 1½" x 55"
Top rail	(1)	¾" x 1½" x 55"
Drawer dividers	(2)	¾" x 1½" x 4"
Drawer guides	(2)	1¼" x 1" x 10⅞"
Drawer guides	(2)	¾" x 1⅞" x 10⅞"
Top fasteners	(12)	9/16" x 1" x 1½"
Drawer parts		
Front	(3)	⅝" x 2½" x 17½"
Back	(3)	⅜" x 2½" x 17½"
Sides	(6)	⅜" x 2½" x 11½"
Bottom	(3)	⅜" x 11 3/16" x 17⅛"
Knobs	(3)	1" x 1" x 1⅝"

CHOOSING WOOD

Look over the wood to be used for the table. Using chalk, roughly mark out the needed parts. Proceed slowly when doing so to decide where the best available grain figure should appear in the table. The visual impact of the finished table depends largely on the layout decisions. Choose the wood for the top first as it is the largest and most visible piece.

LEGS

Refer to the STKM-1, STKM-2, and STKM-3 patterns on page 116. After sawing and planing the legs to the dimensions provided in the part list, decide which two will be the front legs and which way they will face. Mark the faces of the legs that will be mortised. Remember that the rear legs get two mortises, but the front legs are mortised only for the side aprons.

Cut the mortises in the legs with a plunge router and fence. Lay out a mortise on one marked face and then transfer the top and bottom lines to the marked faces on the other legs using a square. Clamp three legs side by side in a bench vise or on the bench to provide a flat surface for the router base. The middle leg of the three is the one that will be mortised, so the first setup will have the leg with the fully laid-out mortise in the middle.

Set the router fence to ride against one of the outside legs. Adjust the router's plunge depth turret to make the full cut in about three steps. Note that the mortises are not centered in the width of the legs; half of them are off center one way and half the other way. All the mortises can be cut with the same fence setting by rearranging the legs in the vise.

Once the legs are mortised, taper them on their two inner sides on the jointer. Lower the infeed table to about a ⅛" cut. Then clamp a stop block on the infeed table so that when the bottom of a leg is butted against the stop block, about 5" of the top of the leg extends past the high point of the cutterhead over the outfeed table. The stop block is only about ⅜" thick to leave room for a push stick to grab the bottom of the leg.

Start the cut by lowering the leg onto the spinning cutter while the foot of the leg is positioned against the stop block. By making repetitive passes in this manner, a taper is created. When both tapers are completed on all four legs, move on to the aprons and rails.

APRONS AND RAILS

Use both the table saw and router table to cut the tenons on the aprons. Cut the shoulders on the table saw. Remove the waste from the cheeks on the router table. Set the height of the cutter on both machines so that a pass on opposite faces will leave a tenon in the middle that is a nice, snug fit in the mortise.

After cutting the tenons, take a piece of coarse cloth abrasive (like a piece of sanding belt) and use a shoe-shine action to round the tenons to fit the routed mortises. A wood rasp also works well. Finally, bevel the ends of the tenons that join inside the rear legs so that the tenons don't interfere with each other inside the mortises.

The drawer rails are the next pieces to fit. Both drawer rails are dovetailed into the front legs, but in different ways. The bottom rail joins with a sliding dovetail, while the top rail joins with a single broad dovetail into the top of the leg.

Cut the sliding dovetail socket by clamping the two front legs together, front face to front face. Clamp a fence across the inside faces to guide a router. Use a ½" dovetail bit and make the socket ½" deep. The center line of this cut must coincide with the center line of the drawer rail.

On the router table, cut the matching dovetails on the ends of the bottom rail. Use a tall fence and a square-cornered backing/pushing board to guide the rail, on end, past the bit. Move the fence to adjust the width of the dovetail for a proper fit in the socket.

The top rail gets flat dovetails. Lay them out with a bevel gauge, cut them on the band saw, and trim the dovetails with a sharp chisel. Reinforce this dovetail with a screw at final assembly.

The drawer opening is divided for the three drawers by double mortising dividers into the top and bottom rails. Measure between the shoulders on the rails so that there are three equal spaces. Mark for the mortises carefully. Drill or rout the mortises in both rails.

Cut the tenons on the dividers to fit by the same procedure as the aprons. Saw out the center so that there is a double tenon. Round the tenons to fit the mortises. Hand-saw a small slot in each tenon 90° to the grain to receive a wedge during assembly.

With rails fitted, measure the openings to make the drawers. The drawers are supported in this opening by two drawer guides screwed to the side aprons with countersunk screws and two center supports doweled to the front rail and back apron. Measure the actual table before cutting the guides to the dimension given in the drawing. Adjust as necessary.

MAKING THE DRAWERS

The drawers have traditional details: half-blind dovetails in the front and through dovetails in the back, French bottom, and a turned knob with a wedged tenon. The bottoms fit into grooves in the front and the sides and are fastened to the drawer backs with a screw. The grain of the bottom panels runs across the width of the drawer and the screw hole is slotted to allow the panel to expand and contract across the grain.

For each drawer, resaw the sides, back and bottom from thicker stock and match the grain. Rout the grooves for the bottom before laying out the dovetails as a reminder to position a tail over the groove.

After the dovetails have been cut, trimmed and properly fit, shape the top edge of the drawer parts with a router to give the drawer a more delicate appearance. Make certain that the drawer is square and sits flat when assembling it to avoid problems when fitting the drawer to the table.

Fit the drawer stops, positioning them so that the drawers are flush with the drawer opening. With the drawers in place, sand the drawer fronts and table front at the same time to ensure that they are flush.

Finally, trim ¹⁄₆₄" from the front edges of the drawer stops so the drawer front is recessed ¹⁄₆₄".

The gap between each drawer front and the table should be even all around the opening. To adjust the gap at the bottom, to match the sides and top, plane only the bottom edge of the drawer front. The plane doesn't touch the bottom of the drawer sides. Slightly round the edges of the drawer and drawer opening with sandpaper.

When turning the drawer knobs on the lathe, include a ⅜" tenon as shown on pattern DKKM-1 on page 107. Saw a groove in the tenon (for a wedge). Glue and wedge the knob into the drawer front. To keep these short drawers from coming all the way out of the table, loosely screw a small turn-cleat to the inside edge of the top rail to act as a drawer retainer. The cleat must be swung up to remove the drawer.

PEG JOINTS

When the table is fully assembled and the glue is dry, pin the mortise and tenon joints with square pegs. Drill two ³⁄₁₆" holes through each joint. Use a ³⁄₁₆" drill to set the distance between the fence and the blade on the table saw, and rip out lengths of ³⁄₁₆"-square peg stock. Square up the tops of the holes with a small chisel and glue in the pegs. Then saw off the excess and pare them flush with a chisel.

Shaker furniture was simple and refined as well as light and portable— serving the communal style of living since all items were owned by the entire society and subject to being moved around.

Open drawer policy. The Sofa Table with drawers open
reveals a wealth of space for storing special items.

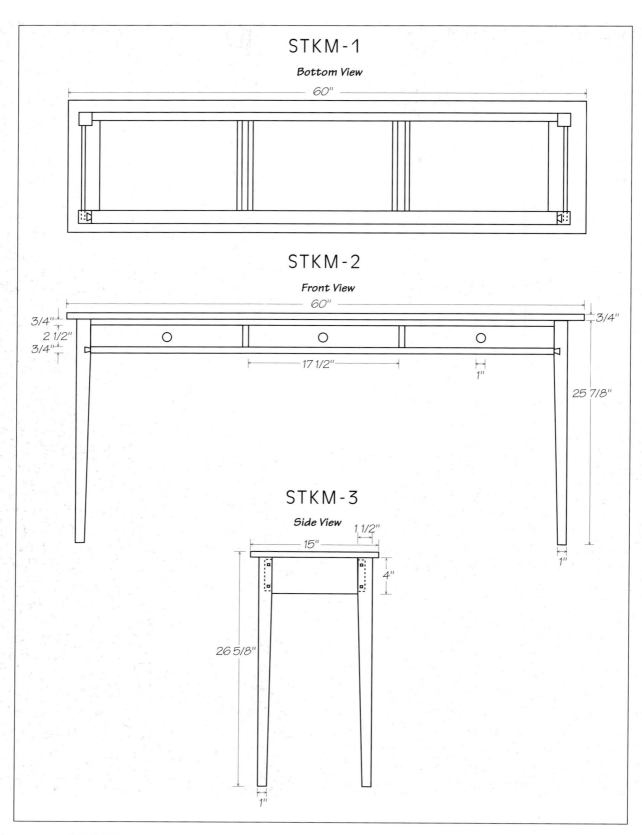

STKM-1

Bottom View

60"

STKM-2

Front View

60"

3/4"
2 1/2"
3/4"

3/4"

17 1/2"

1"

25 7/8"

1"

STKM-3

Side View

1 1/2"

15"

4"

26 5/8"

1"

The art of study. The curly maple Drop Leaf Table is shown
with leaves up and accompanied by two low back chairs.

Drop Leaf Table

by Kelly Mehler

CHOOSING WOOD

Look over the wood to be used for the table. Using chalk, roughly mark out the needed parts. Proceed slowly when doing so to decide where the best available grain figure should appear in the table. The visual impact of the finished table depends largely on the layout decisions. Choose the wood for the top first as it is the largest and most visible piece. The two drop leaves are joined to the top with drop leaf hinges and a "rule joint." To make the rule joint, use a ½" round over bit on each side of the top and a matching ½" cove on the inside edge of the leaves.

LEGS

Refer to the DLKM-1 and DLKM-2 patterns on page 120. After sawing and planing the legs to the dimensions provided in the part list, mark the centers on each end and turn on the lathe. Then mark the face of the legs that will be mortised to receive the two side aprons.

Cut the apron mortises in the legs with a plunge router and fence. Lay out a mortise on one marked face and then transfer the top and bottom lines to the marked faces of the other legs using a square. Clamp three legs side by side in a bench vise or on the bench to provide a flat surface for the router base. The middle leg of the three is the one that will be mortised, so the first setup will have the leg with the fully laid-out mortise in the middle.

Set the router fence to ride against one of the outside legs, then adjust the router's plunge depth turret to make the full cut in about three steps. Note that the mortises are not centered in the width of the legs; half of them are off center one way and half the other way. All the mortises can be cut with the same fence setting by rearranging the legs in the vise.

Cut the double mortises for the bottom drawer rails at the drill press with the legs lifted 3°

APRONS & DRAWER STRETCHERS

Use both the table saw and router table to cut the tenons on the aprons. Cut the shoulders on the table saw, and then remove the waste from the cheeks on the router table. Set the height of the cutter on both machines so that a pass on opposite faces will leave a tenon in the middle that is a nice, snug fit in the mortise.

After cutting the tenons, tack a piece of coarse cloth abrasive (like a piece of sanding belt) and use a shoe-shine action to round the tenons to fit the routed mortise. A wood rasp also works well.

The drawer rails are the next pieces to fit. The top drawer rail joins with a single broad dovetail into the top of the legs and the bottom rail joins with a double tenon.

The procedure for cutting the bottom rail's double tenon is basically the same as on the aprons, except the shoulders end up at 3°. First, cut the tenon at the regular 90° and then mark the angle with a bevel gauge. When marked, hand-cut the angle with a back saw and chisel. After cutting the tenon, transfer the dimensions from the mortises to the tenons. Remove the waste from the center and ends. Then round the two tenons for a snug fit.

The top rail gets flat dovetails. Lay them out with a bevel gauge. Cut them on a band saw and trim the dovetails with a sharp chisel. The shoulders are also cut at a 3° angle. Cut a matching socket in the top of the legs with a back saw and chisel. Reinforce this dovetail with a screw at final assembly.

With the rails fitted, measure the opening to make the drawers. The drawers are supported in this opening by two drawer guides screwed to the side aprons with countersunk screws. Measure the actual table before cutting guides to the dimensions given in the drawing. Adjust as necessary.

MAKING THE DRAWERS

The drawers have traditional details: dovetailed corners, French bottom, and a turned knob with a wedged tenon. The bottom fits into grooves in the front and the sides and is fastened to the drawer back with a screw. The grain of the bottom panel runs across the width of the drawer and the screw hole is slotted to allow the panel to expand and contract across the grain.

For each drawer, saw the sides, back and bottom from thicker stock and match the grain. The front and back of the drawer are sawn at 3° to match the drawer opening. The bottoms of the sides are also cut at 3° so they will sit flat. Rout the grooves for the bottom before laying out the dovetails as a cue to position a tail over the groove.

After the dovetails have been cut, trimmed and properly fit, shape the top edge of the drawer parts with a router to give the drawer a more delicate appearance. Make certain that the drawer is square and sits flat when assembling it to avoid problems when fitting the drawer to the table.

Fit the drawer stops as shown, positioning them so that the drawers are flush with the drawer opening. With the drawers in place, sand the drawer fronts and table front at the same time to ensure that they are flush. Finally, trim ¹⁄₆₄" from the front edges of the drawer stops so the drawer front is recessed ¹⁄₆₄".

The gap between each drawer front and the table should be even all around the opening. Adjust the gap at the bottom to match the sides and top by planing only the bottom edge of the drawer front. The plane doesn't touch the bottom of the drawer sides. Slightly round the

edges of the drawer and drawer opening with sand paper.

When turning the drawer knobs on the lathe, include a ⅜" tenon as shown on pattern DKKM-1 on page 107. Saw a groove in the tenon (for a wedge). Glue and wedge the knob into the drawer front. To keep these short drawers from coming all the way out of the table, loosely screw a small turn-cleat to the inside edge of the top rail to act as a drawer retainer. The cleat must be swung up to remove the drawer.

PEG JOINTS

When the table is fully assembled and the glue is dry, pin the mortise and tenon joints with square pegs. Drill two ³⁄₁₆" holes through each joint. Use a ³⁄₁₆" drill bit to set the distance between the fence and the blade on the table saw, and rip out lengths of ³⁄₁₆"-square peg stock. Square up the tops of the holes with a chisel and glue in the pegs. Saw off the excess and pare them flush with the chisel.

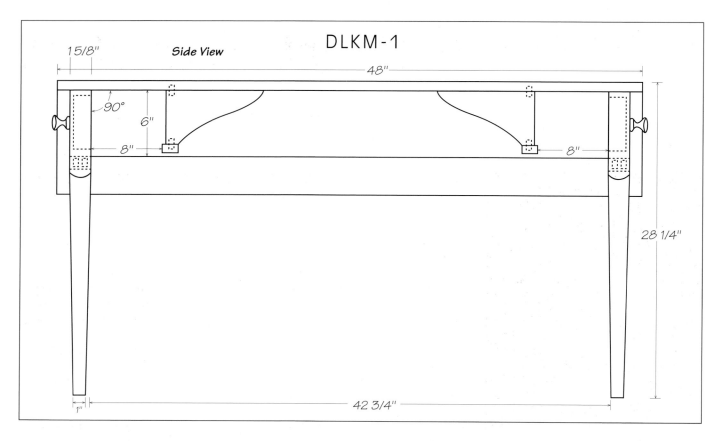

DLKM-1

Side View

15/8"

48"

90°

6"

8"

8"

28 1/4"

1"

42 3/4"

DLKM-2

End View

16 1/2"

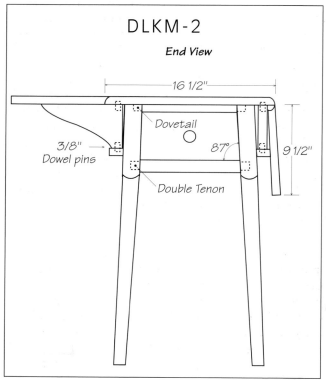

Dovetail

3/8"
Dowel pins

87°

9 1/2"

Double Tenon

Good grain. The Drop Leaf Table is shown from above for a view of the beautiful pattern created by matching the grain.

chapter 4   Robert Wurster:
Profile & Philosophy

photo by Misty Householder

ROBERT WURSTER—A PROFILE

The unusual integrity and beauty of Robert Wurster's work struck me when I first saw it in 1986. Writing about it a decade later, those qualities are what immediately surface to memory. It is reassuring to me that work like his, though not in every home, continues to be made. It encourages the rest of us as we maintain this rare and difficult profession.

Robert makes reproduction, interpretive, and custom furniture in his shop, called Woodworks of Berkeley Springs, in West Virginia. His work has been exhibited in juried shows. His furniture making career, launched in 1981, is en-hanced by his background, which is strong with diverse perspectives: several years using his artistic and creative talents in television production, vocational teaching, and a degree in biology. A semi-professional guitarist, he has naturally put his talents to making instruments too—guitars, ukuleles, mandolins, and hammered dulcimers—though his instruments are not for sale. And, he is such a good writer!

The intensity and thoughtfulness he exudes about his work, complemented by his multi-disciplinary perspective and wider view of life—and a healthy sense of humor—are inspiring. ■

—Robert Sonday

ROBERT WURSTER—PHILOSOPHY

Stop watching TV and get into the shop.

Beginning woodworkers are often hesitant to undertake a complex project because of a lack of confidence in their skills. It is easy to pass on trying a new technique by blaming a lack of proper tooling in the shop. But that is just an excuse. Too many watch the TV guys and sit back thinking, "Yea, I could do that if I had a shop with all of those tools."

The fact is that plenty of the fine furniture around today was built without power tools of any kind. Of course, it would be nice to have that dovetail jig, but a back saw and chisel have served the same purpose for centuries. The tools most important to the typical Shaker cabinetmaker would easily fit into a box that could be carried by one person. The secret to successful woodworking for the amateur is improvisation. If the specific tool is not available, adapt those that are to suit the task at hand.

Don't be fooled by how easy it looks on television. Nobody can build an end table in a half hour—at least not one that is worth having. What the viewer doesn't see is the incredible amount of time that goes into stack preparation and the power tool set-up necessary to

SHAKER WOOD   **121**

accomplish a specific operation. A few buttons pushed in the editing booth sends a half hour of test cutting and tool adjustment into the netherworld of out-takes. In the home shop, the same amount of time dedicated to careful layout and hand cutting will accomplish the same end. Electricity will never be a good substitute for careful craftsmanship.

Another thing the viewer doesn't often see on TV is a mistake, the bane of all human endeavors. The key to success is not to be afraid of errors. Save all off-cuts until the project is complete. A board can't be made longer, but oftentimes it can be made wider by gluing the off-cut back on. Likewise, the off-cut pile can serve as a source for a replacement part, should one be needed.

Break the project down into its constituent components and work on them one at a time. Is the drawer opening in the end table a little too wide? Leaving the drawer construction until last allows for adjusting the dimensions to fit. Is the cabinet glued up a little out of square? Make the door a little larger than the opening and trim it down for an even gap. Mistakes happen. The hallmark of craftsmanship is finding a way through them.

Finally, remember that television is a forgiving medium when it comes to appearances. The poor resolution of the TV screen makes anything look better than it does in real life. Take your time, use your head and the tools at hand, and the project will turn out just fine. ■

Pine Cupboard

by Robert Wurster

SPECIFICATIONS

BASICS

Material: pine
Overall Dimensions: 71½" high x 30¼" wide x 18¼" deep
Finish: tung oil

PART LIST

Pine

Sides	(2)	¾" x 17" x 69⅝"
Case stiles	(2)	¾" x 4¾" x 69⅝"
Case rail	(1)	¾" x 2⅜" x 20"
Door stiles	(2)	¾" x 3¾" x 63¾"
Top door rail	(1)	¾" x 4½" x 14¼"
Middle door rail	(1)	¾" x 7½" x 14¼"
Bottom door rail	(1)	¾" x 5¾" x 14¼"
Door panels	(2)	⅜" x 11" x 23½"
Top, shelves	(5)	¾" x 16⅝" x 25¾"
Back	(as needed)	½" x random widths x 65¾"
Cove molding	(1)	¾" x ¾" x 60"
Bull nose molding	(1)	⅞" x 1⅞" x 60"

CHOOSING WOOD

Chalk out rough outlines of each part needed. Select boards considering their figure, color and physical characteristics. Set aside those with the straightest grain for the face frame and door frame parts. Select boards with the most interesting grain for the door panels. The straightest pieces should be used for the door stiles, as stock that starts out straight and flat will most likely remain that way. This is especially important in door parts if the door is to remain flat. The less-straight or knotty boards can be cut for the smaller parts. The worst stock can be used for shelves and other secondary parts.

Cut the boards into individual pieces, adding a little extra length and width on each, and joint and plane both faces and one edge. The stock is now ready to be cut to final dimension.

ASSEMBLING THE CASE

Refer to the PCRW-1 pattern on page 125. Glue up the side panels and lay out and cut the feet. Machine the rabbet for the back. The shelves can be let into dadoes in the sides, but biscuits provide a more reliable joint. When constructing this large case, glue up only one side at a time. Dry-assemble the remaining side and clamp up the case. Use slightly convex clamping cauls to distribute pressure to the center of the panels.

After the glue has set, remove the dry side, glue, and re-clamp. This method takes very little extra time and greatly reduces the open time for the glue joints and the stress on the crafts person.

Peace in pine. The Pine Cupboard stands ready to hold
the practical or the quixotic treasures of the home.

SHAKER WOOD   **123**

ASSEMBLING THE DOOR

Cut the frame parts to final dimensions. Number the pieces on the plan and label the machined pieces correspondingly.

Cut the tenons. Cut the shoulders on a sliding saw table with a stop block set to provide the correct tenon length. Note that the shoulders of the tenon are offset front and back to allow for the beading around the door panel (PCRW-2 at right). The tenon cheeks are best cut with a tenon jig on the table saw. Drill or rout out the corresponding mortises and square them up with a chisel.

Mill a ¼" round bead on the inside front edge of each piece. Then mill the grooves for the door panels using a router with a ¼" round-over and ¼" slotting bit. Trim and miter the bead at the ends of the stiles as shown on PCRW-2 pattern.

Resaw the lumber for the bookmatched door panels. Make both panels from consecutive pieces of the same board to help integrate the appearance of the door. Cut a rabbet around the back of the glued up panels to create a tongue to fit the grooves in the frame, making certain to allow ⅛" on either side for expansion of the panel in the frame.

Glue up the door in the same manner as the case—one side at a time. Clamping the door to the bench top will ensure that the door stays flat during assembly. Insert panels before gluing up the second side. Apply finish to the door panels and the bead on the frame before assembly; finish that is applied later tends to stick and crack in dry weather.

FACE FRAME

Check the finished width of the door assembly and cut and tenon the top frame rail to ensure that the door opening equals the width of the door plus ⅛". Machine the corresponding mortises in the stiles. Lay out and cut the feet on the stiles. Make the stiles wide enough to allow them to extend over the sides a little—the excess will be planed off later. Because this frame has only a single rail top, it is best to assemble the frame and glue it to the case at the same time.

MOLDINGS

Make the top molding in two pieces, a bull nose with an applied cove. Glue the cove molding into the nosing, and then miter the composite molding at the front corners. Glue the face molding to the case, with the side moldings glued at the miter and secured by screws at the back. Slotted screw holes allow for seasonal movement of the case as shown in the PCRW-3 pattern at right.

BACK

Make the back of ½" random-width stock rabbet-lapped and nailed to the shelves.

PCRW-2

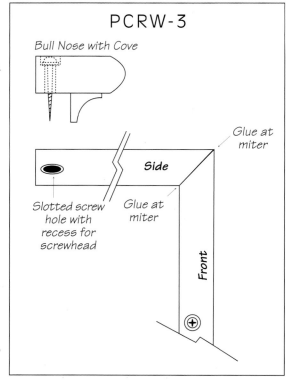

PCRW-3

Bull Nose with Cove

Glue at miter

Side

Glue at miter

Slotted screw hole with recess for screwhead

Front

PCRW-1

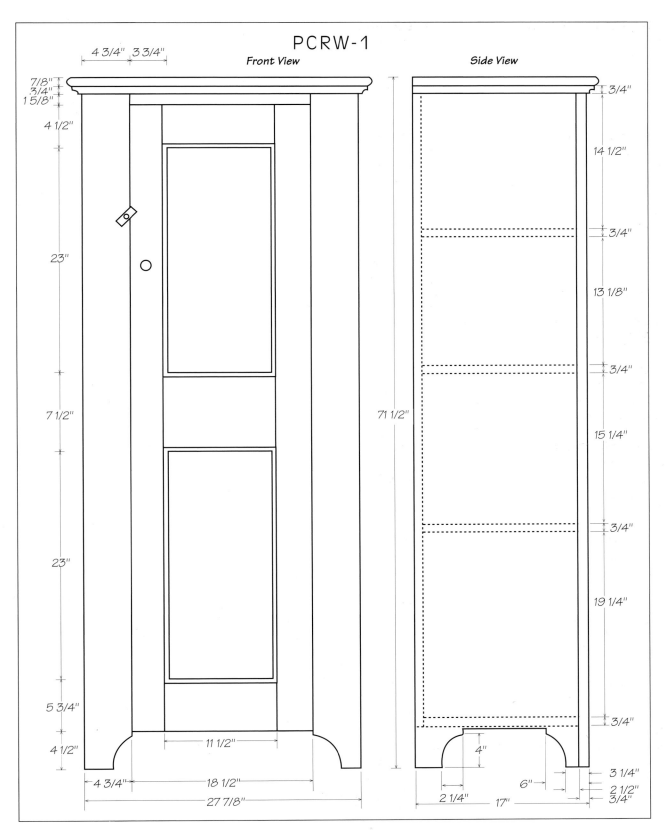

Front View

Side View

Corner Cupboard

by Robert Wurster

SPECIFICATIONS

BASICS

Material: cherry and bird's-eye maple
Overall Dimensions: 72½" high x 27" wide x 12¾" deep
Finish: tung oil

PART LIST

Cherry		
Case stile	(4)	¾" x 3" x 71⅝"
Upper case rail	(1)	¾" x 2⅜" x 20"
Center case rail	(1)	¾" x 3⅞" x 20"
Lower case rail	(1)	¾" x 5⅜" x 20"
Upper door stiles	(2)	¾" x 3¾" x 27¼"
Lower door stiles	(2)	¾" x 3¾" x 32¾"
Top door rails	(2)	¾" x 3⅞" x 13"
Bottom door rails	(2)	¾" x 4⅝" x 13"
Top, shelves	(5)	¾" x 11½" x 28"
Back	(1)	¾" x 6" x 71⅝"
Sides	(as needed)	⅜" x random widths x 71½"
Cove molding	(1)	¾" x ¾" x 36"
Top bull nose molding	(1)	⅞" x 1⅞" x 36"
Center bull nose molding	(1)	⅞" x ¾" x 36"
Base molding	(1)	½" x 3½" x 36"
Bird's-eye maple		
Upper door panel	(1)	⅜" x 10" x 19¼"
Lower door panel	(1)	⅜" x 10" x 24⅞"

CHOOSING WOOD

This piece began with two cherry boards. One was used to make all of the rails for both doors and case, while the other was used for the stiles. The boards were marked and cut to provide the pieces needed to fabricate the case and doors. Each piece was numbered and marked for face orientation. A bird's-eye maple board was used to make book-matched panels for the doors. The end result is that the assembled parts bear the same spatial relationship to each other that they had in the tree. It is extremely important to work carefully, as a ruined piece cannot be easily replaced, but the visual integrity of the finished piece is worth the extra effort.

CONSTRUCTING THE FACE FRAME

Refer to the CCRW-1 and CCRW-2 patterns on pages 129 and 130. Prepare the case stiles, noting that each stile is made up of two pieces mitered together to form the return at either side. It is easiest to cut the mortises for the case rails, the rabbet for the back, and the biscuit slots for the shelves before the two pieces are glued together. Biscuits inserted in the miter joint help keep the two pieces aligned when clamping pressure is applied (see the CCRW-3 and CCRW-4 patterns on page 131 and 130). The biscuit slots are cut at the correct angle by using a jig. Clamping jigs are used to distribute the clamping force during glue up. Use the same jigs to clamp the face frame during assembly, one side at a time as described in the Pine Cupboard on page 122.

ASSEMBLING THE CASE

Lay out the profile for the shelves by standing the assembled face frame on the blank for the first shelf and scribe the inside bottom edge. Cut this first shelf carefully, and then use it as a template for the others. Cut the remaining shelf blanks slightly oversize, clamp the template to each in turn and use a pattern cutting bit in a router to trim them to final dimension.

Cut the biscuit slots in the shelves and assemble them to the face frame. Beveled blocks temporarily screwed to the back edges of each shelf provide a clamping surface. Fasten the cabinet back to the back edge of the shelves with glue and biscuits. Before the glue sets, check to make certain that the shelves are square to the face frame. Use several of the triangles shown in pattern CCRW-5 on page 131 to maintain squareness when gluing up carcases.

INSTALLING THE SIDES

Sides are ⅜" random width boards rabbet-lapped and nailed to the shelves.

Put in the corner. The cherry and bird's-eye maple Corner Cupboard sits
in harmony with the contrasting colors on the Shaker dwelling's walls.

ASSEMBLING THE DOORS

Follow instructions for Pine Cupboard, Assembling the Door on page 124.

MOLDINGS

The top molding profile is a bull nose over a ½" cove. The center molding is a bull nose with a tongue let into a dado as shown in the CCRW-6 pattern on page 131. The baseboard is topped by a ½" round over with a bead. All are mitered at the return breaks on either side of the face frame. Make all smaller moldings by machining the desired profile on the edge of a board, and then ripping the molding off on the table saw. All moldings are glued to the face frame. Small screws are driven into the moldings from inside the case and adjacent to the miters to prevent the minimal seasonal movement that will occur from opening the joint.

Nothing to hide. The open doors of the Corner Cupboard reveal four spacious shelves.

The cupboard is an emblem of the Shakers' insistence on order and cleanliness.

CCRW-1

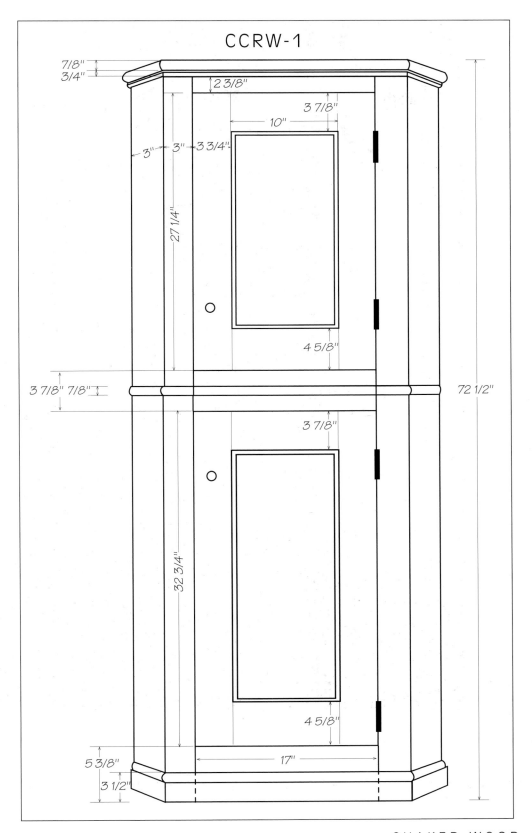

7/8"
3/4"
2 3/8"
3 7/8"
10"
3" 3" 3 3/4"
27 1/4"
4 5/8"
3 7/8" 7/8"
3 7/8"
72 1/2"
32 3/4"
4 5/8"
17"
5 3/8"
3 1/2"

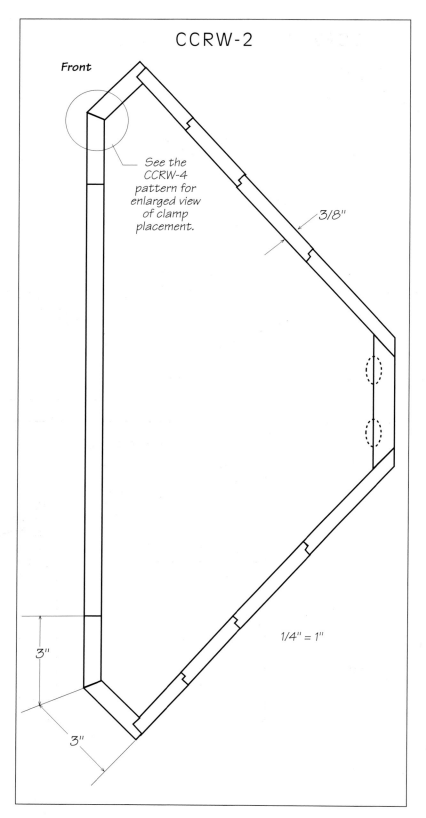

CCRW-2

Front

See the CCRW-4 pattern for enlarged view of clamp placement.

3/8"

3"

3"

1/4" = 1"

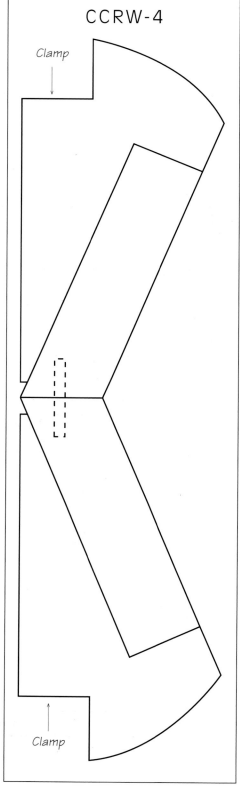

CCRW-4

Clamp

Clamp

CCRW-3

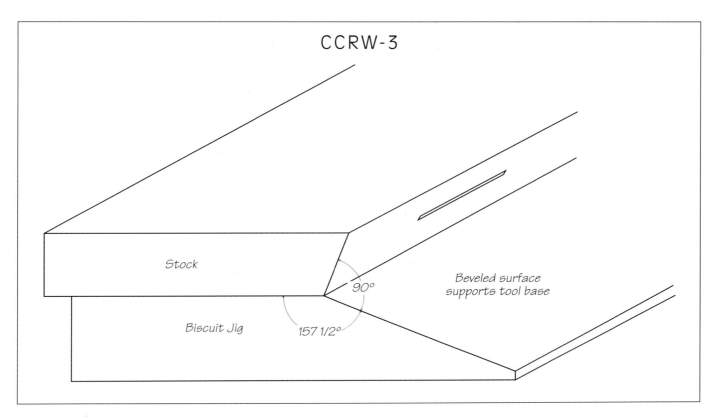

Stock

Biscuit Jig

90°

157 1/2°

Beveled surface
supports tool base

CCRW-5

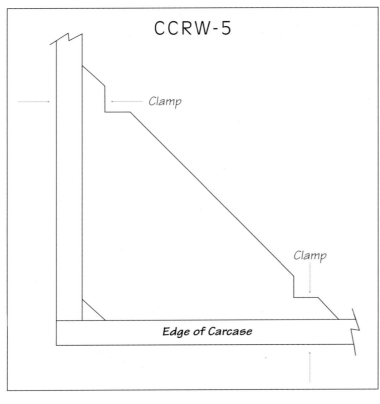

Clamp

Clamp

Edge of Carcase

CCRW-6

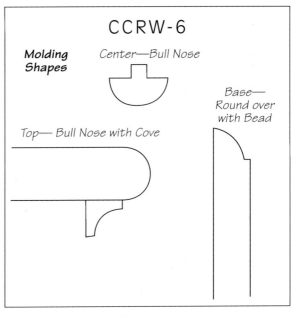

***Molding
Shapes***

Center—Bull Nose

*Base—
Round over
with Bead*

Top— Bull Nose with Cove

Open invitation. The walnut Footed Table welcomes the passerby inside.

Footed Table

by Robert Wurster

SPECIFICATIONS

BASICS
Material: walnut and pine
Overall Dimensions: 27⅛" high x 27⅞" wide x 17½" deep
Finish: tung oil

PART LIST

Walnut		
Legs	(2)	⅞" x 3⅝" x 20⅞"
Feet	(2)	⅞" x 7½" x 16⅛"
Cross braces	(2)	⅞" x 1⅝" x 16½"
Stretcher	(1)	1" x 1⅝" x 28¾"
Top	(1)	½" x 17½" x 28⅞"
Drawer runners	(2)	¼" x ⅜" x 7"
Drawer front	(1)	1 1/32" x 2 5/16" x 21¾"
Pine		
Drawer sides	(2)	1 1/32" x 2 3/16" x 7⅛"
Drawer back	(1)	1 1/32" x 1¾" x 21¾"
Drawer bottom	(1)	5/32" x 7" x 21⅜"

FTRW-1

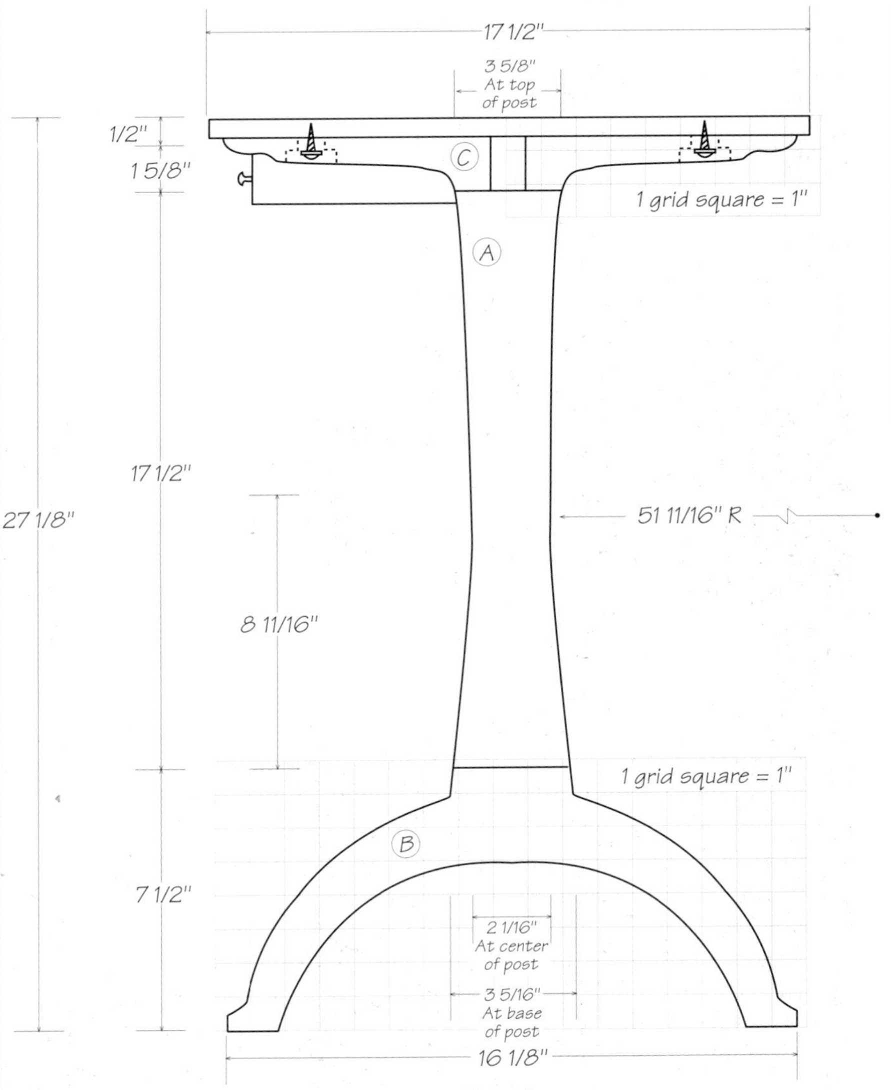
17 1/2"
3 5/8" At top of post
1/2"
1 5/8"
C
1 grid square = 1"
A
17 1/2"
27 1/8"
51 11/16" R
8 11/16"
1 grid square = 1"
B
7 1/2"
2 1/16" At center of post
3 5/16" At base of post
16 1/8"

Side View

INTRODUCTION

This table is a walnut copy of a cherry original that is now part of the collection of the Fruitlands Museum located in Harvard, Massachusetts. The patterns for this piece are based on drawings from the *The Book of Shaker Furniture* by John Kassay, published by the University of Massachusetts Press.

BASE

Refer to the FTRW-1 pattern at right and the FTRW-2 pattern on page 135. The joinery for the leg assemblies is best accomplished on squared stock. Cut the curves of the legs and the feet after all of the necessary machining is completed. Use quarter sawn stock for the feet to prevent warping.

Cut the mortises in the feet, the cross brace stock, and the tenons on the legs. The notch in the cross braces and top leg tenons will be cut after they are assembled. Make a template of the foot-leg-cross brace profile from poster board and trace the outline onto the work piece. Disassemble the parts and cut to shape on a jig saw or band saw. Cut carefully, paying particular attention to the points where the separate parts meet.

Smooth the cut edges with sandpaper, except for the areas around the joints. Then reassemble with glue and clamp. The unsanded areas at the joints can be sanded after the glue has set.

Saw the ends of the stretcher to shape. Smooth them with sandpaper. Cut the notches in the stretcher and legs with a back saw and chisel, taking care to make the bottoms of the notches flat, as that is the primary glue surface. Drive a screw through the stretcher into the leg tenon to strengthen the joint.

Glue and screw the drawer runners to the inside of the cross braces.

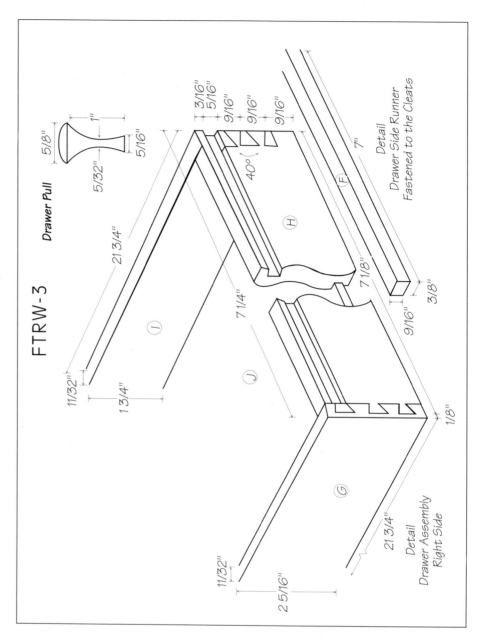

CONSTRUCTING THE DRAWER
Using the FTRW-3 pattern at right, lay out and cut the dovetails in the drawer sides first. Then use the sides as templates to trace the ends of the pins directly onto the ends of the corresponding drawer face or back. Rout the groove in the drawer sides, for the drawer bottom. Pre-sand all the drawer parts, and then assemble the drawer with glue.

DRAWER PULL
Refer to the FTRW-3 pattern above. Turn the drawer pull out of scrap stock.

TABLE TOP
Refer to the FTRW-1, FTRW-2 and FTRW-4 patterns on pages 133 and 135. Make certain to apply finish equally to both sides of the top to prevent warping. Drive screws up through the cross braces to secure it to the base, allowing for screw head travel during seasonal movement.

FINISH
Apply four coats of oil and then one coat of wax.

FTRW-2

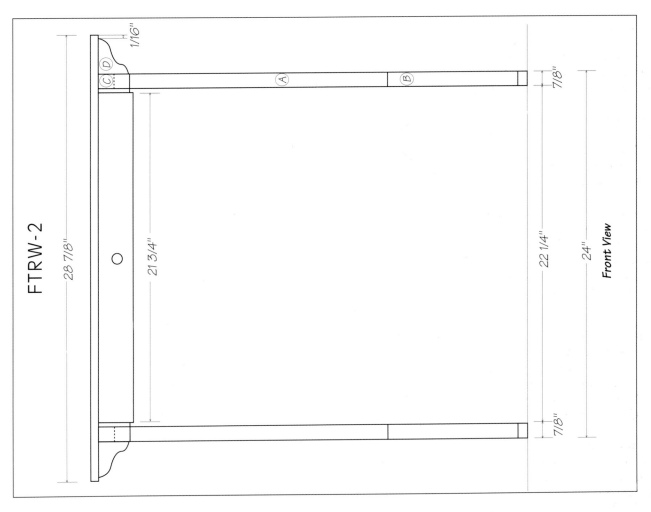

1/16"

28 7/8"

21 3/4"

7/8"

22 1/4"

24"

7/8"

Front View

FTRW-4

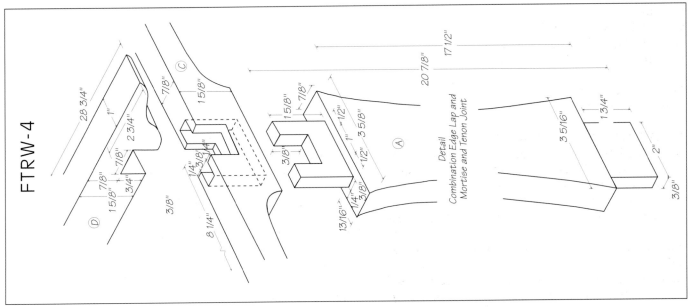

28 3/4"
1"
7/8"
2 3/4"
7/8"
1 5/8"
3/4"
3/8"
8 1/4"
1/4"
3/8"
7/8"
1 5/8"
17 1/2"
20 7/8"
1 5/8"
7/8"
3/8"
1/2"
1"
3 5/8"
1/2"
1/4"
3/8"
13/16"
3 5/16"
1 3/4"
2"
3/8"

Detail
Combination Edge Lap and
Mortise and Tenon Joint

Settee

by Robert Wurster

SPECIFICATIONS

BASICS
Material: maple and white pine
Overall Dimensions: 33" high x
 15½" deep x 61¼" long
Finish: tung oil

PART LIST
Maple

Front legs	(2)	1½" dia. x 17½"
Back legs	(2)	1½" x 18"
Stretchers	(2)	1³⁄₁₆" dia. x 13¼"
Back rail	(1)	⅝" x 4" x 61¼"
Spindles	(19)	1¹⁄₁₆" dia. x 13⅞"

Pine

Seat	(1)	1½" x 14" x 61¼"

INTRODUCTION

This settee is a reproduction of an original that is now part of the collection of the Philadelphia Museum of Art. The patterns for this piece are based on drawings from the *The Book of Shaker Furniture* by John Kassay, published by the University of Massachusetts Press.

SPINDLES & LEGS

A duplicating lathe or the help of someone who has such a machine is very useful for this step.

Referring to the SERW-1, SERW-2, and SERW-3 patterns on pages 138–140, turn the legs, spindles, and stretchers to the specifications in the part list. Use straight grain stock for the spindles and make a few extra, in case any split in the bending process. Make the tenons slightly fatter than specified to allow for a tight fit. Just before assembly, compress the tenons by twisting them into the correct size hole drilled into a maple block. When glue is applied and the parts are assembled, the tenon will swell slightly, assuring a tight fit.

BEND THE SPINDLES

Make a simple steaming chamber from a piece of 3" or 4" PVC pipe as shown in the SERW-4 pattern on page 140. Stand the pipe up in a pan of boiling water, drop in the spindles, cover the pipe and let them cook for 30–45 minutes. Remove the spindles, one at a time so they stay hot, and bend them into the bending jig, as shown in the SERW-5 pattern on page 141, with the growth rings perpendicular to the dowels in the jig to prevent splitting. A ¹⁄₁₆" wooden shim between the spindle and the jig dowels prevents dents in the spindles. Set aside to dry for several days.

CARVE SEAT

Rip the white pine plank for the seat from to the correct width, leaving the ends square, and draw the seat profile on each end. The bevels at the front and back are cut first on the table saw. The rest of the profile can be roughed out with a core box bit in a router fitted with an edge guide.

Rout a series of grooves the length of the seat, resetting the edge guide to move the router over and adjusting the depth of cut to the profile drawn on the ends of the plank for each pass. Shift the router over far enough to leave a strip at full thickness every few inches to provide support for the router base.

Use a sharp plane to smooth out the grooves on the convex part of the profile. Make each pass with the plane run the full length of the seat to ensure an even surface. A convex plane is the best choice for smoothing the concave part of the profile. However, the task can also be completed using a small convex spoke shave and goose-neck scraper.

Turn the seat over, lay out the curves for each end and cut to shape with a saber saw. Use the largest 45° chamfering bit available to continue the bottom bevel around each end as shown in the SERW-6 pattern on page 141. Saw and pare off any excess stock that the bit doesn't reach. Work from the top with chisel and rasp to round the ends down to the edge of the bottom bevel. Finish up by smoothing the seat with progressively finer grades of sandpaper.

BACK RAIL

Mill the back rail blank. Then lay out and drill the spindle mortises along one edge. Cut the taper by shimming the edge of one face with a ³⁄₁₆" strip of wood (use double-stick tape) and running the rail through the surface planer. Flipping the rail end for end and repeating the process with a ⅜" strip provides a corresponding taper on the second side.

DRILL MORTISES

Use special carriages clamped to the drill press table to hold the leg at the correct angle for the stretcher mortises as shown in the SERW-7 pattern on page 142. Use simple shop-made drill guides for the leg and spindle mortises.

The guide for the seat mortises to receive the spindles is made from maple stock, 1" x 2" x 60". Lay out the spindle spacing along the 1" face and drill a series of ⅜" holes all the way through. Rip an 85° bevel along the 1" face. Clamp the guide to the seat with the beveled side down and drill through the holes into the seat.

The guides for the seat mortises to receive the front and back legs are made in similar fashion, using maple blocks 2" x 3" x 8". Drill the guide hole in the exact center of the block and mark the centers of the ends and sides of the block. These marks will aid in positioning the guide for use. The bevels for the front and back guides are 88° and 75° respectively. Test the drill guides and jigs on scrap stock before using them on the finished parts.

GLUE SPINDLES AND LEGS

Check fit on each piece before applying any glue. Slight bevels on the ends of all tenons will aid in getting them started into their respective mortises. During assembly, apply glue sparingly to the sides of the mortises and more liberally to the tenons.

Assemble the legs and stretchers first. Then install the assemblies to the seat by starting the back legs in first and pounding the ends of the legs alternately to get them seated.

Glue and insert the back spindles one at a time into the seat. Work quickly to get the spindle seated and the bend oriented correctly before the glue "grabs."

Install the back rail, once dry, to get a feel for the process. Start at one end, progressively feeding the ends of the spindles into the holes. Some spindles may need to be trimmed to length. Glue applied to five or six of the spindles will be sufficient for the final assembly.

Classic comfort. The maple and white pine Settee provides soothing contours and eye-pleasing angles.

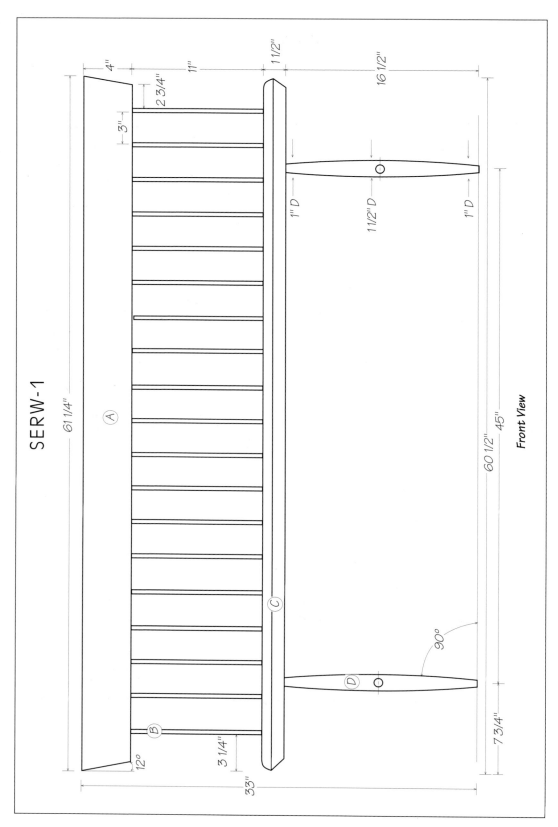

SERW-1

Front View

SERW-3

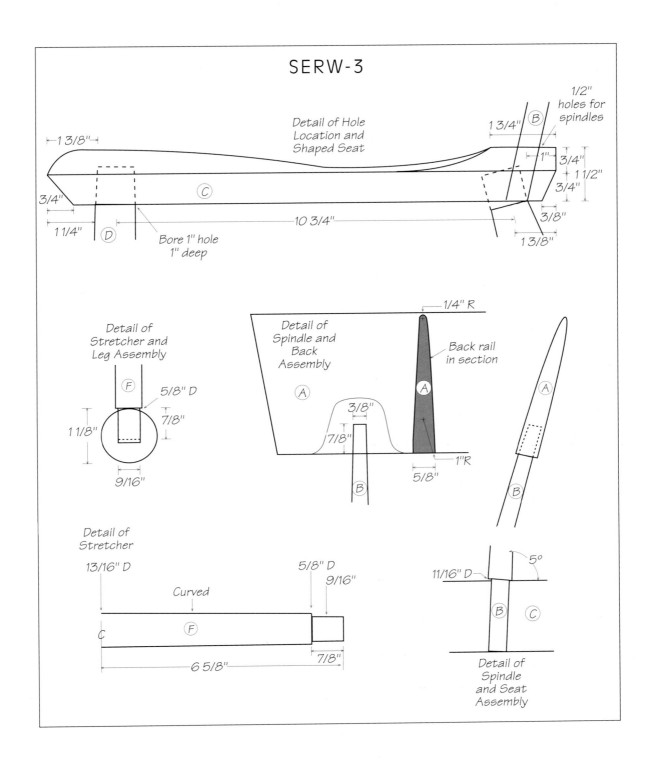

Detail of Hole Location and Shaped Seat

1 3/8"

1 3/4"

1/2" holes for spindles

B

1"

3/4"

1 1/2"

3/4"

3/4"

C

3/8"

10 3/4"

1 1/4"

D

Bore 1" hole 1" deep

1 3/8"

Detail of Stretcher and Leg Assembly

F

5/8" D

7/8"

1 1/8"

9/16"

Detail of Spindle and Back Assembly

A

1/4" R

Back rail in section

A

3/8"

7/8"

B

5/8"

1"R

A

B

Detail of Stretcher

13/16" D

Curved

5/8" D

9/16"

C

F

6 5/8"

7/8"

11/16" D

5°

B

C

Detail of Spindle and Seat Assembly

SERW-2

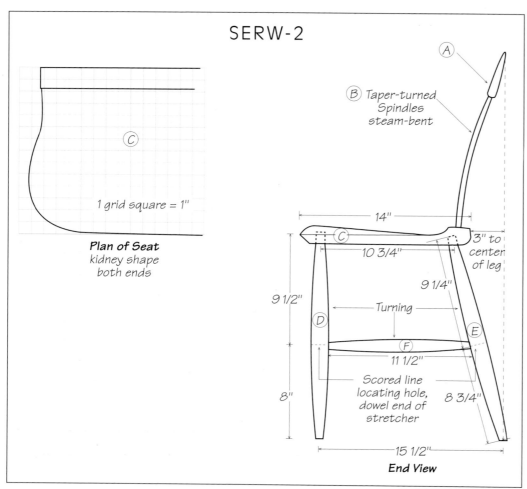

1 grid square = 1"

Plan of Seat
kidney shape
both ends

(A)

(B) Taper-turned
Spindles
steam-bent

14"

(C)

10 3/4"

3" to
center
of leg

9 1/4"

9 1/2"

Turning

(D)

(E)

(F)

11 1/2"

Scored line
locating hole,
dowel end of
stretcher

8"

8 3/4"

15 1/2"

End View

Shaker furniture is delicate but sturdy. It was treated with great care by Believers who recognized in their possessions not private property to be abused, but communal property to be shared with future generations of Shaker converts.

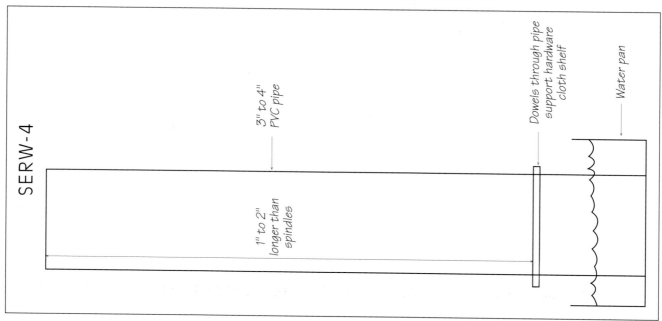

SERW-4

3" to 4"
PVC pipe

1" to 2"
longer than
spindles

Dowels through pipe
support hardware
cloth shelf

Water pan

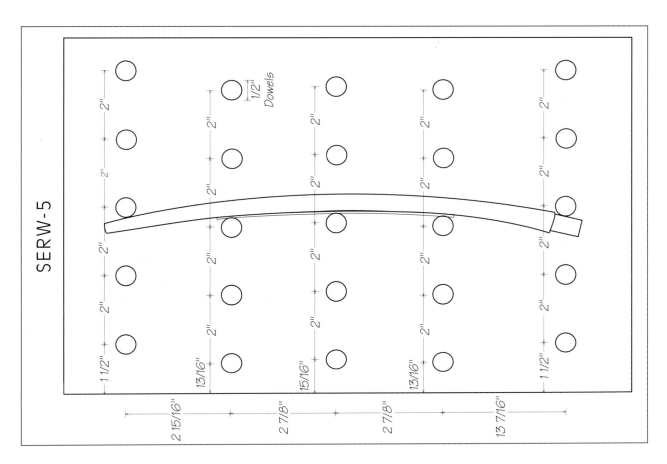

SERW-5

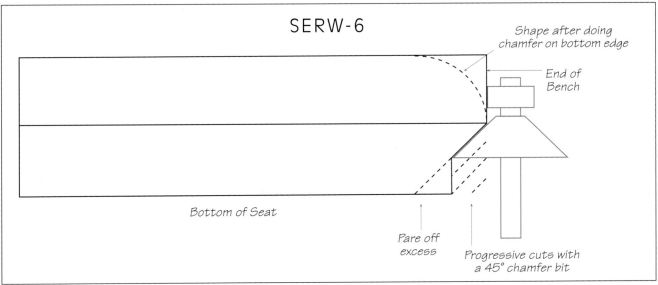

SERW-6

Shape after doing
chamfer on bottom edge

End of
Bench

Bottom of Seat

Pare off
excess

Progressive cuts with
a 45° chamfer bit

The Shaker adventure here is over, but the story remains of their life and labor.

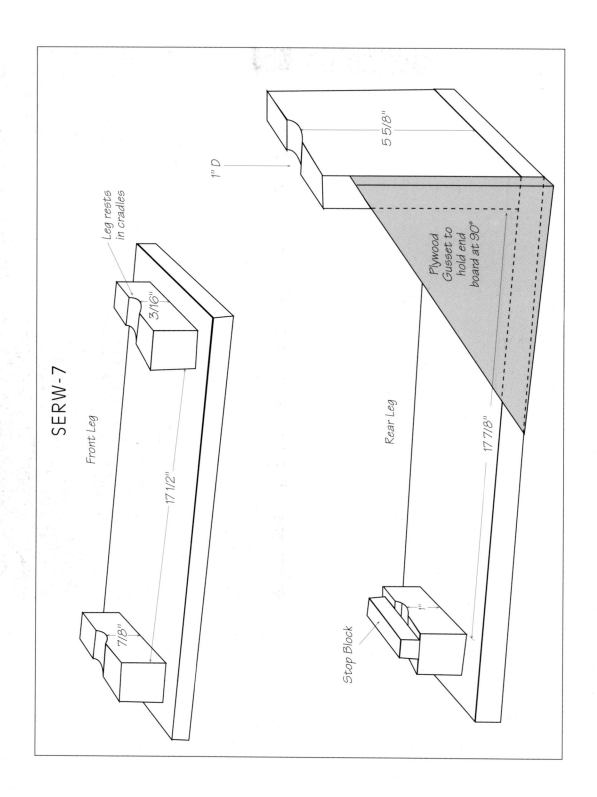

SERW-7

Front Leg

Leg rests
in cradles

3/16"

7/8"

17 1/2"

1" D

5 5/8"

Plywood
Gusset to
hold end
board at 90°

17 7/8"

Rear Leg

Stop Block

1"

■ index

metric equivalency chart

MM-Millimetres   CM-Centimetres

INCHES TO MILLIMETRES AND CENTIMETRES

INCHES	MM	CM	INCHES	CM	INCHES	CM
⅛	3	0.3	9	22.9	30	76.2
¼	6	0.6	10	25.4	31	78.7
½	13	1.3	12	30.5	33	83.8
⅝	16	1.6	13	33.0	34	86.4
¾	19	1.9	14	35.6	35	88.9
⅞	22	2.2	15	38.1	36	91.4
1	25	2.5	16	40.6	37	94.0
1¼	32	3.2	17	43.2	38	96.5
1½	38	3.8	18	45.7	39	99.1
1¾	44	4.4	19	48.3	40	101.6
2	51	5.1	20	50.8	41	104.1
2½	64	6.4	21	53.3	42	106.7
3	76	7.6	22	55.9	43	109.2
3½	89	8.9	23	58.4	44	111.8
4	102	10.2	24	61.0	45	114.3
4½	114	11.4	25	63.5	46	116.8
5	127	12.7	26	66.0	47	119.4
6	152	15.2	27	68.6	48	121.9
7	178	17.8	28	71.1	49	124.5
8	203	20.3	29	73.7	50	127.0

YARDS TO METRES

YARDS	METRES	YARDS	METRES	YARDS	METRES	YARDS	METRES	YARDS	METRES
⅛	0.11	2⅛	1.94	4⅛	3.77	6⅛	5.60	8⅛	7.43
¼	0.23	2¼	2.06	4¼	3.89	6¼	5.72	8¼	7.54
⅜	0.34	2⅜	2.17	4⅜	4.00	6⅜	5.83	8⅜	7.66
½	0.46	2½	2.29	4½	4.11	6½	5.94	8½	7.77
⅝	0.57	2⅝	2.40	4⅝	4.23	6⅝	6.06	8⅝	7.89
¾	0.69	2¾	2.51	4¾	4.34	6¾	6.17	8¾	8.00
⅞	0.80	2⅞	2.63	4⅞	4.46	6⅞	6.29	8⅞	8.12
1	0.91	3	2.74	5	4.57	7	6.40	9	8.23
1⅛	1.03	3⅛	2.86	5⅛	4.69	7⅛	6.52	9⅛	8.34
1¼	1.14	3¼	2.97	5¼	4.80	7¼	6.63	9¼	8.46
1⅜	1.26	3⅜	3.09	5⅜	4.91	7⅜	6.74	9⅜	8.57
1½	1.37	3½	3.20	5½	5.03	7½	6.86	9½	8.69
1⅝	1.49	3⅝	3.31	5⅝	5.14	7⅝	6.97	9⅝	8.80
1¾	1.60	3¾	3.43	5¾	5.26	7¾	7.09	9¾	8.92
1⅞	1.71	3⅞	3.54	5⅞	5.37	7⅞	7.20	9⅞	9.03
2	1.83	4	3.66	6	5.49	8	7.32	10	9.14